Award-winning investigative journalist Gavan Naden started his career as a photographer at Racecourse Technical Services and was at the finish line when Burrough Hill Lad won the Cheltenham Gold Cup in 1984. Gavan has written for the *Guardian*, *Express* and *Mirror* newspapers.

Max Riddington was born in Leicester and lived for over twenty years in a farmhouse alongside a feisty Arab gelding and two sedate Welsh mountain ponies. She has written for *The Times*, *Guardian* and *Daily Mail*.

BURROUGH HILL LAD

THE MAKING OF
A CHAMPION RACEHORSE

GAVAN NADEN AND
MAX RIDDINGTON

First published in the UK by Chequered Flag Publishing
PO Box 4669, Sheffield, S6 9ET
www.chequeredflagpublishing.co.uk

A CIP record for this book is available from the British Library

Printed in the EU by Print Group Sp. z o.o.

ISBN 9780956946065

All photographs courtesy of Stan Riley

Gavan: For Holly and Oscar.
Max: For Tom, my boy.

FOREWORD

As I sit here in my air conditioned office overlooking the magnificent King Abdul Aziz Racecourse, I can't believe it's thirty years since I was lucky enough to be on board the mighty Burrough Hill Lad heading for victory in steeplechasing's Blue Riband, the Cheltenham Gold Cup. It was my mother's sixtieth birthday and she is still going strong. How different my life is today in the 40 degree heat of Saudi Arabia!

I first got to know Burrough Hill Lad when he came to Jimmy Harris' yard and I was his conditional jockey. I have a lot to thank Jimmy for as he got me started and it was under his guidance that the horse won his first race at Market Rasen.

Unfortunately for Jimmy, Burrough Hill Lad's owner, Stan Riley, moved the horse to Harry Wharton. Fortunately he still wanted me to ride him. It was my first association with Harry and I went on to ride a good few winners for him over the years. Harry only ran the horse twice and both times he won with him, at Uttoxeter and Cheltenham. I remember the Cheltenham win – he beat Richdee of Captain Crump's and he was still only a four year-old.

However, Stan moved the horse once more, this time south to Jenny Pitman. I had never ridden for Jenny before but Stan said he would like me to continue riding Burrough Hill Lad. At that time I was based in the north with trainer Mick Easterby and wasn't always available but I remember riding Burrough Hill Lad in his first Novice Chase at Leicester.

He then ran at Newton Abbott, but I had other commitments and Colin Brown of Desert Orchid fame rode him and won. Colin rode him twice more but unfortunately parted company with him both times, including in the Sun Alliance Novice Chase at the Festival. I was back on board when he won the first of his major races at Aintree in the Mildmay Novice Chase. I then rode him at Newton Abbott on Easter Monday and was rewarded with yet another win.

The following season, Burrough Hill Lad was thrown in with a featherweight in the Welsh National. I was riding a lot of winners for Scottish trainer Harry Bell and so, through loyalty to him, I rode Lasobany at Chepstow. I pulled up and Burrough Hill Lad bolted up in the hands of John Francome. He then kept the ride until he went on to partner Brown Chamberlin at Cheltenham.

After that I knew he was turning into a decent horse – but things don't always go as you expect.

About three weeks before the Cheltenham Festival, I was riding at Sedgefield for Gordon Richards on a horse called Welfare and at the last fence in the back straight had a fall and broke my nose. My great friend and colleague Alan Brown said, 'Bloody hell Tuckie, I wouldn't say you've bust your nose but you're smelling through your left ear!' I was operated on by a surgeon in Middlesbrough and when I came out of hospital, Burrough Hill Lad was winning the Jim Ford Chase at Wincanton.

It then became touch and go to get fit in time for Cheltenham. Around this time, BT were running a television campaign for shares in the company with a character called Buzby, which was Burrough Hill Lad's nickname, and it seemed nearly every jockey in the country was ringing Jenny for the ride on Burrough Hill Lad. But luckily I was back in the saddle a couple of weeks later.

Probably due to all the bangs on my head, I don't remember much about the parade ring chat other than we were going to sit handy in the race, but I do remember Jenny saying, 'Make sure you jump the third last.' The race went according to plan and I sensed we were going to win. Brown Chamberlin was jumping out to his right and so I stuck to the inside rail and we stormed up the hill together with a fantastic feeling of power. But even after I knew we had won, I still waited for the Judge to say, 'First, number four.' The reception we received was incredible, especially as there had been rumours that all was not well with the horse.

There's a tradition in the weighing room that the horse's name is written above the jockey's peg where he got changed and then he signs his name. I would like it to go on record that it was one of the valets who misspelled the horse's name and not me!

I was unable to join Maria and all my family and friends for immediate celebrations as I was riding in the County Hurdle for Bill Stubbs. Once finished, the other tradition is that the winning jockey buys champagne for the boys in the changing room. I did this and then went off to the bar. As I arrived my great friend Will Lefebvre, who used to work for the Press Association, called to Stan that we needed more champagne! He replied, 'No thanks, I've had enough.' That night I took ten people to dinner in Winchcombe.

The following season I started off riding Burrough Hill Lad at Cheltenham and ended up in the stewards' room because they thought I had been too easy on him. Explanations were accepted that he needed the run, a fact that Jenny made no secret of, and he duly went on to win at Wincanton. I was then replaced by John Francome in the Hennessey Gold Cup.

I remember riding for Jenny at Leicester when the news of my replacement broke and recall going to Stan and saying, 'I'm sorry you have reached the decision you have, but I think I am man enough to take it and I wish you the best of luck at Newbury.' Maybe that's why I was back on board to ride him to victory in the Charlie Hall Chase at Wetherby in his next race.

The following year, in the lead up to Cheltenham, Jenny asked me to ride Burrough Hill Lad in the Greenall Whitley Breweries Handicap Chase. John was needed elsewhere but I had committed to ride Earls Brig for Billy Hamilton, who I was going to ride in the Gold Cup. I explained the situation to Billy and being the gentleman he said, 'If it benefits your career, ride Burrough Hill Lad at Haydock and you can still ride Earls Brig at Cheltenham.' In the end, John rode Burrough Hill Lad at Haydock, but I won the race on Earls Brig.

Today, I am a Stewards' Advisor for the Equestrian Club Riyadh, and have been here just over eight months. What an experience my wife, Maria, and I are having. I am working with wonderful people and it is great experiencing different cultures and customs. When John Sanderson of International Racecourse Management asked if I would be interested in the job, I jumped at the opportunity of returning to the stewards' room environment. At the time I was Clerk of the Course at Sedgefield, a place I knew only too well as it was where I broke my nose just three weeks before the Gold Cup!

I retired from race riding at Newcastle in February 1990 with a final win on Midland Glenn for trainer Les Eyre, having achieved a total of 423 winners which almost pales in to insignificance compared to today's jump jockeys. But not all of them will be privileged enough to win a Gold Cup, and for that I am thankful.

I've been involved in the sport ever since and consider myself extremely lucky. I have loved it and got paid for it to boot. I can't think of anything else I would rather have done. If I could have my riding career over again, I would – with the proviso I'd make fewer mistakes. I've still got a scar below my right eye from a kick at Southwell in 1978, and my nose is bent from the break before the Gold Cup. I came out looking like Darth Vader! The surgeon who operated on me inspected it after removing the plaster cast and said, 'If you were an actor I would set it again, but seeing as you're a jump jockey you'll probably get it kicked back the other way!'

As for Burrough Hill Lad, he was truly a magnificent animal and it was my privilege to be part of his career. Sadly Jimmy Harris and Harry Wharton are no longer with us. While I haven't spoken with Jenny for some time, I have no doubt she is, like my mother, still going strong.

Phil Tuck
Riyadh, 2014

PROLOGUE

Kempton. 18 January 1980. 3.30pm.

It was almost over before it began.

Twelve weeks after the black gelding's first ever race, his owner, trainer and stable lad all look down at the ground. Then at each other. Then they shake their heads.

The horse is lying prostrate on the turf, not moving, barely twitching. He had tried to leap the last hurdle but smacked his back legs and somersaulted in the air. The ground rose up before he could correct himself. Landing on his neck he took a massive blow, over 1500 pounds smashing at 30 miles per hour onto the track. Enough force to crumple the front of a car, enough speed to kill a pedestrian. Jockey Steve Knight scrambled away from the cascading muscle, flesh and hooves, desperate to save himself. He thanks God he had the agility to roll away. He sees the horse on his side, stunned, unable to make a sound.

Amidst the sodden turf and dank sky, there is an eerie silence. Even the applause is muted as a little known horse called Corbiere thunders through the finish line in first place.

Then a rumble of concern comes from the stands, eyes look back to where the horse has fallen.

The injured beast is massive at 16.3 hands, his heart the size of a volleyball pumping at over a gallon every single second. Adrenalin whips round his broken body, heat rising from his flanks. Will he ever amount to much? Not if he doesn't get up, jokes some wag.

As the seconds turn to minutes, even the joker falls silent. This looks bad, really bad.

Steve Knight knows he should have won, but at that last hurdle everything went into slow motion. 'One moment he was clear, the next he fell in a heap.' He remembers the ground being soft, the horse slowing and the hurdle rising up in front of them like a giant monolith.

The horse had started gently on two cylinders, then bang, his head dropped, his neck swelling as oxygen surged through his body. When the shoulders popped out, Steve was thinking, 'Christ! I'm on a different bloody horse!'

It takes some courage to ride him. You have to know his secret: the moment when both ears go flat back. Then the turbo kicks in, his stride so big the ground is a blur. That's when you hold on for dear life.

Twenty lengths ahead and heading towards that last hurdle, round the tight right-hand Kempton bend, nothing can beat him now, thought Steve. Except all that muscle and power just kept motoring towards the obstacle, like it didn't exist. When those ears drop he just wants to run flat out. He doesn't care what's in his way. That's how it happened. 'He fell into the fence, more or less collapsed into it.'

Now the horse looks seconds from death.

Steve moves carefully towards the horse's side and tries to undo his girth. He can see his shallow breathing. The stable lad is running towards them yelling, 'Is he ok?'

Now what? Do we get the gun?

Trainer Jimmy Harris is keeping his fingers crossed. This is a horse that could write history. A beast with amazing potential, he'd seen it from the off. This horse is so strong, he can run all day; a real trier, with pace. What more can you ask from a black beauty with a temperament to match?

When hope is almost gone, the four year-old suddenly snorts and a shiver runs down his body.

'He's moving!' A voice calls from the stands. 'He's bloody moving!'

Slowly but surely the horse rises to his feet. Shaky legs struggle to find a footing. He's on all fours but can't lift his head, his neck twisted at a strange angle, almost touching the ground. Stunned, in pain, but refusing to give up.

They lead him back to the horsebox and gently encourage him on board. The light is fading. If he isn't going to give up, neither can they.

They know this one is special.

They know him as Buzby. Everybody else knows him as Burrough Hill Lad.

1

Charles Ernest Riley gathered his family around the wireless on one cold Friday in March 1927 to listen to the first ever horse race broadcast on the radio. A monotone voice cracked and rose excitedly as the final stages of the Grand National penetrated the static.

Ernest, as he preferred to be known, ticked off the list of runners in his newspaper. His name suited him perfectly: a strong, sometimes gruff man, horses were a part of his farming life. But he had a dream – to one day own an animal that could be raced like Mary Partridge's horse, Sprig, who'd just won the world's most famous steeplechase. It had taken the owner three attempts. She refused to give up, determined the horse would one day win in memory of her son, who died in action weeks before the end of the First World War. Mary's inspirational tale was without doubt a great victory for persistence and honour.

For Ernest, the story brought mixed emotions. There was glory and dignity in giving your life to defend the shores of Britain. His duty had been to work the land and feed a nation at war. His life was safe, yet it gave him no great joy.

The Government had exempted farmers from conscription because they were more useful to the nation in their usual job. So Ernest did as he was told and undertook his role with a seriousness that pervaded his whole personality. Farming was in his blood and Burrough on the Hill in Leicestershire was the only world Ernest had ever known. Further back than he could remember, for nearly 200 years, his family had worked the land. His debt to the men on the front line would be paid in sweat and toil.

He was a proud father to two young sons who would continue the family legacy, and he had another child on the way.

On the morning of Wednesday 27 April 1927, you could hear a pin drop in Cheseldyne House's normally noisy kitchen.

The boys had been dropped off at their Grandma Riley's at Newbold Farm, a mile up the road. They'd been sent packing by their mam to play with the farm's newly born kittens. In the peace and quiet of the scullery, Lucy

May Riley dragged the dolly tub's cumbersome steel barrel over the stone floor. Today was washday and being six months pregnant wasn't going to stop her doing the chores. How could it, with a busy husband and pair of inquisitive sons to care for?

There was an inevitability about Lucy May's life – it was highly unlikely she would marry anyone other than a farmer. A dairymaid and daughter of a rural labourer from Langham, she had grown up near Oakham on the Leicestershire-Rutland border. Her mother was long gone and her father had died just the year before. He left her nothing, most likely because he had nothing to leave. Without parents to guide her and a family of her own to raise, she had developed a tough outer skin. She married Ernest and made the best of their lives together, meaning every word of her vows, 'Till death us do part.'

Now in her thirties, she was feeling exhausted. As she wearily twisted the sheets with the dolly's clawed pole, she promised herself a moment's rest. First, she hauled the sodden laundry from the barrel and carefully fed it through the mangle, squeezing out every last drop of water. When the sheets were finally billowing on the line, her arms ached, but she took pleasure in another job well done.

She welcomed the local shopkeeper and handed him a few coppers as he dropped off a fresh loaf from his Somerby store. A moment later she was distracted by a noise coming from the cooking range, laughing when she realized it was only her new kettle that had begun to whistle.

Soon Ernest would return from a morning's ploughing ready for a brew.

She edged past hams hanging from the beams and stirred the cauliflower soup simmering on the hob. Ernest loved caullies and this year there was a good crop in the vegetable garden. He'd seen off the pesky rabbits with netting sheets and snared the more determined blighters. It was a time of waste not, want not, and Ernest always looked forward to her hearty rabbit pie.

Lifting the heavy iron kettle from the stove, a violent pain stabbed Lucy May's body. Her pregnancy had so far progressed with customary ease, just like the previous two; although she wondered if this time she might bear a daughter, someone to keep her company and share the domestic load. As the contraction increased, she gripped onto her pinafore and clenched her teeth. 'Not now,' Lucy May muttered. She feared the worst – a child born two months too soon would have little chance of survival.

Lucy May carried on laying the table even as the pains continued. The sound of her husband's footsteps trudging up the path brought momentary calm.

The muscles on Ernest's sinewy arms bulged as he carefully carried a bucket of water drawn from the well towards his waiting wife. Up since dawn, he'd spent the morning milking the cows and checking the hedges. He couldn't afford to lose any sheep. April had proved wet and inclement, heralding a miserable start to spring. The farm needed a little less gloom and a little more warmth.

He placed the bucket next to the sink as his wife clutched onto the back of a kitchen chair, her face ashen and contorted in pain.

'Fetch the nurse,' Lucy May said, 'and hurry!' This baby was coming whether they liked it or not. Ernest turned heel, yelling at her not to worry, and leapt on his fastest horse in search of Nurse Mills. 'Please don't let her be out on another call,' he murmured under his breath, urging the beast to gallop ever harder towards Somerby.

Lucy May was biting down on a wooden spoon when Nurse Mills arrived on her bicycle. A few minutes later, Lucy May gave one final push and a tiny squeal echoed round the room, more suited to a piglet than a baby.

An hour later the doctor, John Mould, stood puffing on his pipe, shaking his head gravely. This was such an early birth he doubted the little scrap weighing just two pounds would live more than a few hours. He imparted the news kindly, saying he hoped the mite had it in him to defy the odds. With such immature lungs his chances of survival were slim and it was unlikely the baby boy would see nightfall. If by some miracle he got through the first few days, he could well be weak and affected for the rest of his life.

The baby was swaddled tight against the cold and settled into a drawer, which was used as a cot. Lucy May stared at the little bundle, hoping against all odds this baby had something of a fighter about him. She heard the doctor's instructions to stay in bed for two weeks to recover and gently raised her eyebrows. Did he really expect a farmer's wife to stay off her feet at the start of spring?

Ernest ushered the doctor down the narrow flight of stairs, pushing coins into the man's smooth palm and promising as many fresh eggs as he could eat. He then waved his hand towards the front door, the threshold used only by the professional and the visitor, where Dr Mould's chauffeur patiently waited outside.

Thoroughly overwhelmed by the day's events, Ernest collapsed into a chair by the iron bedstead while his two other sons peeked through the stair's banisters. He pointed towards their brand new brother and encouraged them forward.

Guided gently by Grandma Riley, Albert, aged four, and Kenneth, aged two, walked gingerly through the gloom of the oil-lit room towards the drawer and peered inside. They both gasped in unison at the tiny baby, sleeping soundly. Grandma Riley smiled and counted out half a dozen freshly laundered hankies to use as nappies.

The constant battle with nature had long defined their lives. Farming was a gruelling business requiring long hours and extraordinary dedication. For the Riley family, birth was just another trial.

Although a harsh existence, the Rileys were better off than most and fortunate to have a large woodpile by the fire, plenty of eggs from the hens and enough bacon for breakfast to make mouths water. Ernest would withdraw his sharpest knife to cut a pig's throat as if it was the most natural thing in the world.

'There's no room for sentiment in farming,' became Ernest's war cry. He worked every daylight hour and often into the night to make the most of his farm. Anything less would be tantamount to failure.

With the Great War years behind them, he dreamed of brighter days and a better future for his sons – unlike the lot of Lucy May's brother, Alfred, who had returned from the trenches a broken man and was now living in one of their outbuildings. The horrors of mustard gas still lingered and he was suffering the terrible ravages of tuberculosis – the poor man's disease. Ernest didn't hesitate to help out. 'Family first,' he said.

Doctors hoped fresh air and good food would heal Alfred's failing lungs, but each night Lucy May fell asleep listening to his hacking cough and awoke to see his sweat-soaked sheets out to dry.

With a sense of foreboding, Ernest knocked on the outbuilding to tell Alfred news of his nephew's arrival. He wasn't answering and Ernest feared the worst. But Alfred finally managed to drag himself to the entrance and listened as it was explained there was a fair chance the baby may not survive. Perhaps Lucy May would bring the tot by in a few days time. 'He might even have a name by then,' Ernest joked.

'Don't let her wait too long,' urged Alfred.

And despite doctor's orders to the contrary, less than 48 hours after giving birth, Lucy May was out of bed and showing off her newborn son.

Alfred raised a smile and said, 'Ah, boy, I don't know who will go first, you or me.'

Lucy May bit her lip at the prospect of also losing another of her beloved siblings. Seven years before, her baby brother Robert died at the tender age of 20 and still to this day she missed him.

It was then she knew. The name that had eluded her now became crystal clear.

If the new baby survived, he would be called Robert.

Six weeks later, the child, despite all gloomy predictions, was gaining weight and thriving. Lucy May was not doing so well. The dark circles beneath her eyes deepened each day and showed no sign of fading. Her new son was a demanding mite who fed little and often, morning and night. There was little time for sleep. Thankfully, the evaporated milk that supplemented Lucy's breastfeeding was helping make him strong.

Grandma Riley stopped by every day to help Lucy May with the chores and the children. Being devoutly religious, she advised her daughter-in-law to hurry up and get the baby welcomed into the church family.

On a cloudy day in June 1927, they gathered in the beautiful thirteenth-century village Church of St Mary. Spirits were high and the pews filled quickly for a special Sunday service. Today the bell ringers created a sound that lifted the hearts of the congregation.

One of the Riley ancestors, George Porter Riley, had been so taken by the sound, he immortalised the chimes in a poem.

The old church bells of Burrough,
How beautifully they ring,
Fit for Nobleman to hear,
Fit for Queen or King.

The baby, swamped by the family's christening gown, was carried in the arms of Lucy May and gently handed to Rector Gedon who solemnly uttered the words, 'I baptize you, Robert Stanley Riley,' as he poured water over the baby boy's tiny head.

The celebrations continued back at Cheseldyne House with friends and family tucking into a delicious spread and Grandma Riley's favourite fruit cake, mindful to avoid making a mess of their Sunday best.

Yet within a few weeks the celebrations were a distant memory and the baby had been renamed. Lucy May, upset by the constant references to her deceased brother, could no longer bear to hear his name. It was all too much. She decided the baby from now on should be called Stan, a popular name, meaning stony meadow.

Ernest could finally breathe easy and boast that he had three sons to one day help run the 200-acre farm. After the drama and upset surrounding Stan's birth, that was a great comfort. At the back of his mind he never forgot how lucky they were.

A few years before, five of his cousins from the neighbouring village of Twyford had died in their early twenties, all stricken down by a flu pandemic that targeted young fit adults in the prime of their lives. Having endured the bleak war years only to be felled by something seemingly innocuous was too cruel. This was no ordinary bug – the rate at which the influenza spread alarmed health officials. They had little idea how to contain the outbreak and advice to the general public was scant. 'Discharges from the nose and mouth should be destroyed, if possible in a clean rag or paper, which should then be burnt.' Some victims coughed until their abdominal muscles tore and blood foamed from their mouths and noses. No one felt safe. A generation that had already suffered was being dealt yet another devastating blow. Doctors later learned the virus killed almost 50 million people, more than died in the trenches during the First World War.

And tragically on 1 November, just a few months after her baby's baptism, Lucy May was in mourning once more when Alfred finally succumbed to the ravages of his tuberculosis.

Worryingly for Lucy and Ernest, their eldest son, Albert, also showed signs of illness. He coughed and wheezed after very little exertion and they couldn't help but go easy on the boy. Eventually he was diagnosed with asthma, a disease that experts said could be cured with psychoanalysis and perhaps a cigarette or two. Albert was encouraged to get plenty of fresh air and turn his mind to outdoor activities. He loved horses and found his vocation riding lumbering work horses at the farm or donkeys and ponies from the village. He developed a real flair, showing himself to be a natural horseman.

Albert's regular route was past Burrough Court, a large country house half a mile outside the village, home to Lord Marmaduke and Lady Thelma Furness, an extrovert avant-garde American with a love of Africa. Marmaduke, the first Viscount Furness, charmed his wife with exotic wild animals brought back from his many overseas adventures, most notably a giraffe, a zebra and a porcupine. He hoped these extravagances would rekindle the dwindling affections of his wife and initially thought he'd succeeded when Lady Furness took to riding through the grounds on the zebra, taking great delight in being photographed. However, by 1933, they were divorced and she was engaging in secret liaisons with none other than the future King of England, Edward VIII, right under the noses of the villagers of Burrough on the Hill.

Lady Furness first met the Prince of Wales at a grand ball in Mayfair and again at the Leicestershire Agricultural Show in 1929. There followed a series of regular trysts and a not-so-discreet safari holiday to East Africa in the early part of 1930, while she was still married to Marmaduke. Within a few months, Edward and Thelma met at every available opportunity at Burrough Court.

The opulent surroundings of the manor house really were the perfect place for a party. The jet set of the day were attracted by country pursuits such as fox hunting, especially with Leicestershire's prestigious Quorn, Belvoir and Cottesmore hunts.

It seems remarkable that nobody spotted the Prince of Wales slipping into a side entrance at Burrough Court, bodyguards in tow. However, Thelma and Edward managed to contain the potential scandal within its four walls. Or so they thought.

Thelma made one fatal mistake. In January 1931 she introduced her close friend, Wallis Simpson, to the Prince. Edward had flown himself to Burrough in a twin-engined Dragon Rapide, keen to take part in the following day's hunt. Yet by the end of the evening he had other things on his mind and was transfixed with the enigmatic American divorcee. Within a few months Thelma was history in the Prince's affections. Breakfasting on fresh coffee and his favourite peaches, he was seen wandering the grounds of Burrough Court arm-in-arm with Mrs Simpson.

Unbeknownst to anyone, this grand country house was the seat of change that set in motion a chain of events to forever alter the British monarchy. Edward VIII declared to a shocked radio audience in his abdication address on 11 December 1936, 'You must believe me when I tell you that I have found it impossible to carry the heavy burden of responsibility and to discharge my duties as King as I would wish to do without the help and support of the woman I love.'

Ernest and Lucy May, unaware they were neighbours to history in the making, listened to the broadcast in disbelief. Things like that just didn't happen in Burrough.

2

Young Stan didn't want to get out of bed. Not when he could see his breath condensing in the air around him. He snuggled under the blankets, just his nose poking out in the stark freezing bedroom. Working a twelve hour shift was the norm on the farm and he'd usually go to bed exhausted. Falling asleep was never a problem provided his mum remembered to light the tiny candle on the landing. Although Stan was confident with the farm's biggest horses and most stubborn cows, he was afraid of the dark – sometimes so afraid he'd leap into bed with his big brother Albert, just to have someone close by. Once asleep he was out for the count and it took more than his mother's strident tone to get him up.

Stan eventually dragged his aching body downstairs, eyes half closed as his senses succumbed to the delicious smell of fried bacon from the kitchen.

There were no rest days in the Riley household. Weekday or weekend, animals needed feeding and the land tending. And when the sheep were lambing, Stan was almost comatose with fatigue. Then his eyes would close before his head hit the pillow, knowing he would be dragged out again just a couple of hours later, having to squint across the yard in the early morning darkness towards the barn where the ewes were in labour. He'd learned quickly that life was tough and moaning got you nowhere.

Despite generations of Riley tenant farmers before him, Stan wasn't sure it was the path he wanted to follow. It was always a niggle at the back of his mind. From an early age, he had been an inquisitive child with a real sense of adventure. But to change direction, he would first have to cross his formidable father.

When it came to business, Ernest didn't have time for pleasantries or pats on the back. Life revolved around the animals and the farm. That was the way it had always been. Everyone had to get stuck in and woe betide anyone who failed to do their best.

Being the youngest and small for his age made no difference; Stan still had to pull his weight. His father could see that the tiny scrap of a baby was growing up strong and could be put to good use. Yet it wasn't just his muscles that were developing; Stan had determination and dreams to match.

If truth be told, Stan was more like his dad than he cared to admit. Maybe that was the real reason they didn't always see eye to eye. Even so, rows were few and far between because Stan was never one for confrontation. It was an era when it was normal to respect your elders, and when he didn't agree with his dad, he was simply too scared to say.

This particular morning in November 1940, Ernest growled as Stan stifled a yawn while staggering into the kitchen. He looked at his son's sleepy face and slapped his hand hard on the table. Stan almost jumped out of his skin and quickly checked the clock to make sure he wasn't late. That would be unforgivable.

'Did you hear them?' Ernest asked, glancing out of the window.

'Hear what?' Stan replied, tucking into a rasher of crispy bacon.

Ernest shook his head, incredulous. 'You joking lad? Surely it woke you up?'

Stan shrugged.

Ernest manhandled him into the sitting room. 'It's a wonder we weren't all killed in our beds,' he said. 'Look at the soot that's come down the chimney!'

It had been a particularly dark night and German aircraft seized the opportunity to fly in unnoticed. They swooped down so close to Burrough on the Hill that practically all residents had been woken by the terrifying noise of the droning planes. Targeting strategic locations such as Coventry's military factories and Leicester's Lockheed Brake factory, the Luftwaffe bombers dropped tons of explosives. Coventry Cathedral was soon ablaze, destroying over half the building, homes were reduced to rubble. As they turned tail and flew back to Germany, they launched five more bombs in a straight line towards Stan's village.

It was a huge shock for the rural Leicestershire people who assumed they were miles from the Luftwaffe's aim. The area had been officially deemed safe for evacuees. Luckily for the Riley family, the German pilots miscalculated the bombs' flight path and dropped them too early. That error undoubtedly saved the Riley home in King's Lane from a direct hit. The first bomb hit nearby, killing a couple of cows in a field, while the other four completely missed their targets. Ernest wryly noted his son's enviable ability to enjoy a good night's sleep during an air raid.

In the latter part of the war, the neighbouring village of Somerby was chosen as the covert testing ground for Operation Market Garden, the daring 1944 airborne attack on Arnhem. The surrounding landscape bore such close resemblance to the Dutch town, it provided a perfect training ground.

Six hundred men from the 10th Parachute Battalion were stationed at Somerby and Burrough, preparing for one of the most dangerous raids in history. The battalion not only worked hard (there were sixteen cancelled operations before the lift to Arnhem), they also played hard.

With many Land Girls billeted nearby, romance proved a good distraction from what lay ahead.

It's thought the grandiose Burrough Court burnt down in February 1944 due to overexcitement on the part of the regiment, fed up with twiddling their thumbs and desperate for excitement. Some of the 10th Battalion allegedly used explosives to blow down the doors of the late Lord Furness' well-stocked wine cellar, sparking a blaze which quickly spread. In total, over 150 bottles of alcohol went missing from the cellar. The finger of suspicion inevitably pointed towards the soldiers.

During the commotion, others from the battalion cast aside their personal safety and dashed in to save much of the ballroom furniture. They were seen hauling out the grand piano, placing the magnificent instrument on the lawn in front of the collapsing building. Rather than let the moment go to waste, one of the airmen, Alec Wilson, defied the heat and made a theatrical decision.

Alec, an ordinary lad from Devon with an extraordinary talent, was a classically trained pianist. After circling the grand, he prised open the lid and belted out boogie and dance band tunes, then threw in a few American standards for good measure. Some of the airmen were so taken by his playing they took it in turn to lean against the piano and sing along to the music!

Despite the best efforts of fire crews from Oakham, Loughborough and Leicester, who had to pump water from almost a mile away to douse the flames, the blaze razed the beautiful building to the ground. So much smoke poured from the burning building the plume could be seen from miles away a day later.

Seven months after the strangely melodious fire, the Somerby skies were again filled with smoke. This time it was a convoy of badly damaged allied planes returning from Arnhem. Stan was sitting astride a trailer heading towards Cheseldyne Farm after a hard day in the fields when suddenly the sky was filled with a tumultuous din.

Many of the aircraft struggled home with holes in their fuselage and sections blown away, evidence of a terrible dogfight. Some didn't make it back at all; many of those that did used every ounce of their combat training to survive. There were, said Stan, at least a dozen planes 'with bits of metal hanging off their wings and tails limping back to base'. In that moment, Stan appreciated how lucky he was to merely feel tired. For now at least, the Rileys were safe. Ernest said a silent prayer of thanks that his three sons were by his side.

The conflict had a profound effect on Ernest in a practical respect – demands that Britain become more self-sufficient generated a seismic shift in farming productivity. Advances in yields were not just helpful but absolutely necessary, and Ernest was swept up in an agricultural revolution of epic proportions.

Before 1939, Britain imported around 70% of its food and 90% of its grain. Farming methods were still labour intensive, slow and virtually medieval. English grain was expensive and considered inferior. Huge quantities of American and Canadian wheat were shipped into ports and transported to every corner of the country. It defined an era known as the Grain Invasion, when Britain was dependent on imports to make even the most basic of foods like bread.

Cheap grain produced by countries dubbed the bread-basket nations took away any incentive for British farmers to invest in modern machinery. The war alerted politicians to Britain's major vulnerability – it couldn't produce enough food to feed its own people.

With the threat of German U-boats, shipping grain across the Atlantic became increasingly dangerous and it was feared Britain would be starved into submission. Something had to be done, and fast. The War Cabinet met in secret and drew up a classified report, detailing how the country would deal with the imminent food shortages. Rationing became a reality.

The government demanded farmers plough up pastureland, reduce livestock and grow grains and mixed crops. To encourage participation, farmers would be paid for every acre turned over to cultivation. It was anticipated one and a half million acres of land would be needed and a £2 per acre ploughing up subsidy was proposed. For most, it was an offer too good to refuse.

It was during these frantic years that Stan built an affinity with the work horses. While ploughing furrows and planting crops, Stan became attuned to the way horses moved, how they reacted in different weathers, what kept them working for him. Alone in the fields day after day, he built a rapport with the giant shire horses and they became reliant on each other to get the job done. He learned to coax the very best out of them; they repaid his encouragement with loyal service and a gentleness that belied their size.

The new farming rules did, however, signal the end of one particular passion for Ernest. Although he enjoyed his food as much as the next man, there was one thing he absolutely adored: Stilton cheese, the riper the better.

Ernest had learned to make his own, using a recipe courtesy of Lucy May's dairymaid skills. Stilton making is considered an art form in this part of Leicestershire, to many the spiritual home of the pungent cheese. The rich, open land meant cattle could produce an excellent supply of milk and the cheese's distinctive blue colouring and strong flavour made it very popular. Ernest simply couldn't get enough of it.

Just up the lane, fellow tenant farmer Frank Fryer woke his children early every day and ushered them to the dairy where their small hands were perfect for a vital part of the production.

'There was a square board with hoops on top to make sure the cheese kept its shape. Before we dashed off to school we turned the cheeses every morning and took off the hoops so the whey could drain out,' said his son, Bill. 'My sister Mary Elizabeth and I allowed the blue vein to come through naturally, we didn't use copper wires or anything like that – it just developed with time.'

Each week, baskets of cheeses were loaded up and sent to the spires of Oxford where the dons of Brasenose College eagerly awaited their arrival. 'They were packed in a wicker basket and protected with straw. We'd stitch on the wicker lid with cord and dash down to the station at John O'Gaunt. From there they headed for Oxford.'

However, it took 136 pints of milk to make a single cheese. With the country in conflict, there was little room for such extravagances and the government ordered farmers to cut back on cheese and concentrate on the basics – growing oats, wheat and barley.

During this period of intense activity, Ernest was badly gouged by a heifer and had to rely more on his sons to do the farm work. Ironically, the new government plan proved to be a blessing in disguise. Ernest received nine tractors from the Ministry of Agriculture to help convert pasture land into crops. Stan was greatly relieved. He didn't care if he never saw the runny cheese on the dining room table ever again. Watching his father eat it, maggots crawling out, had put him right off!

Stan's boyhood interests were fast spreading beyond farming and he wanted to develop new skills. He already loved riding and now couldn't wait to get behind the wheel of one of the new tractors. A quick learner, Stan needed only to be shown once, although there was one major obstacle with the tractor: at only just over four feet tall, young Stan's legs were too short to reach the pedals.

Ernest came up with an ingenious solution. He sat Stan in the driver's seat and measured the distance from his toes to the pedals. Disappearing into one of the outbuildings, he took out his saw and cut up a couple of four-inch blocks of wood. He then attached the wood to all the pedals. At first Stan felt it was like walking on stilts, but once he got used to it he happily drove up and down the fields, carting wheat to the stack, all under his dad's watchful eye. Health and safety was a fairly relaxed affair in those days, all that mattered was getting the job done so it was all hands on deck – or in Stan's case, all feet!

Stan grew to love the powerful machines. It was much more fun than helping his mam. Fetching water from the well for the weekly wash wasn't exactly demanding and it wasn't very exciting either – apart from the time he caught his fingers in his mam's mangle after being a little too inquisitive. 'That really, really hurt,' he complained, dashing back to the fields to round up the horses only to be teased by his older brothers for not even being able to do women's work.

Stan was completely exonerated when a few months later he saved the day in heroic fashion.

Lucy May had been washing clothes and trying hard to get the stains out of the boys' overalls. She lit the copper, completely unaware that Ernest had brought several cans of fuel to store inside the house.

Petrol was rationed during the war and the Government had ordered red dye to be mixed with commercial petrol to curb black market sales. But Ernest, like many others, was desperate to circumnavigate the restrictions and created his own illegal stash... in the kitchen!

With the copper now alight, the petrol fumes caught fire and the whole lot shot up in flames. She panicked and ran into the yard, screaming 'Fire! Fire!' at the top of her voice,

'We thought the house was going up,' said Stan, who quickly organised a human chain to collect buckets of soil from the garden. He threw the heavy clay soil onto the fire to dampen down the flames. He then rushed back into the yard and led all the frightened animals away from the smoke and heat, no easy feat. But he knew how important the horses were to the farm.

Stan was soon earning a reputation for his horsemanship. Although never formally taught to ride, he simply caught on watching how his father and older brothers mounted up and rode away. The rest was down to natural talent and confidence.

'I was already filling haynets, mixing feeds and mucking out,' said Stan. 'It was a matter of teaching yourself. I learnt to put the tack on as soon as I could carry it and then it was a case of getting on and hanging on, keeping my heels down and staying on for as long as I could.'

Stan wasn't scared, no matter their size or temperament. Even the heavy horses used for ploughing, hay carting and harrowing would do as he ordered. Stan emulated his older brother, Albert, who although not so naturally gifted at sports, was quite brilliant with horses. Albert spent all his spare time in the stable or with the blacksmith and never missed a local point-to-point, not just to race, but to study the horses' form. Inevitably, Stan tagged along.

Stan soon rode with a competency well beyond his years and it wasn't long before news of his prodigious ability spread beyond the village. A landed military gent and owner of Burrough Manor House, Major Bourne, frequented the local point-to-points and had seen Albert and Stan compete. On a visit to Cheseldyne Farm to ask for help with a shoot, he stopped for a while to admire young Stan riding with confidence round the yard.

After a few words of small talk with Ernest, the Major pointed to Stan and said the young lad was the perfect build for a rider: lean and wiry, but also strong. Ernest nodded, wondering where this conversation was headed.

'He should be a flat jockey,' said the Major.

Ernest was taken aback by the proposal, but also fiercely proud. The Major persisted while Stan jumped off his horse and ran over to where the two men were deep in conversation. He heard the Major offer to provide all the funding needed to train Stan as a jockey. This would include sending the young lad away to school, where his education would also be paid for.

Ernest shooed Stan away. 'If you've finished all your chores I can find you some more,' he threatened. Once Stan was well and truly out of earshot, he turned his attention back to the Major.

'We'll have a think about it,' Ernest said, shaking his hand.

Stan scurried off, not quite believing what he'd heard and wondering what his future held. His father said nothing about the day's events but was quieter at the supper table that evening. Stan knew better than dare ask any questions about Major Bourne's visit. That night sleep didn't come easy; his imagination ran wild with excitement. Was he really about to become part of the Sport of Kings?

Next day, Ernest called Stan into the kitchen. With no sign of emotion, he said, 'You're not going.'

Stan stared at the floor while his father snapped, 'I need you here, working on the farm. This is where you belong. And I won't discuss it further.'

Ernest's word was law; there was no point in arguing. At least he'd been given a moment to dream. It was ironic that Ernest's smallest child had grown to play such a key part in the family business. His strength, character and work ethic were valuable assets Ernest could ill afford to lose. Stan became a victim of his own success.

Yet Ernest's stubbornness made Stan strive quietly for more independence. He now took every chance he could to get out and about in the cart and buggy. The opportunity to escape, clear his head and see more of the world was something Stan looked forward to, even if the adventure was only to the neighbouring village of Newbold. Here he'd pick up Granny Riley and escort her back to Burrough Post Office so she could cash in her weekly pension, then worth the princely sum of ten shillings.

He was photographed not long after riding a little further afield through Melton Mowbray, trying to raise money for the Red Cross. As a member of the Young Farmers, Stan is atop a dappled pony, wearing a long white gown with a cross on his right lapel, looking for all the world like a junior doctor. Many of the tiny villages dotted across the county raised money for the charity, which provided essential medical care before the days of the National Health Service.

Such community spirit was second nature and people united in the face of adversity. In his younger days, Ernest helped with an appeal for the Memorial Hospital in Melton Mowbray by winning a tug of war competition. He kept the 1928 winner's medal tucked away in the corner of a drawer with an overwhelming sense of pride.

The war effort demanded new levels of stoicism. With a common enemy, everyone pulled together. Ernest's twelve cows produced milk for the entire village. Milking them was a long laborious job taking well over an hour.

For a while, Stan flirted with the role of junior milkman. Issued with pint and half pint measures and a churn filled to the brim with freshly drawn milk, he crisscrossed the village, knocking on all the doors, filling jugs and jotting down how much everyone owed. And at the end of every week he'd return to collect the money. It was something he enjoyed, and it presented him with an opportunity. When he spotted his big brother Albert enviously eyeing up his sugar ration on the kitchen table, Stan realised there was more money to be made. Never possessing a particularly sweet tooth, he wasn't bothered by sugar in his tea. But he did enjoy making a few extra bob.

'How much will you give me for it?' Stan asked, tantalisingly pushing the sugar packet forward as if it were a wad of money in a poker game.

Albert emptied his pockets of pennies and Stan smiled to himself. Now this was the sort of education he preferred – formal instruction at the village school bored him rigid.

His headmistress, Miss Edith Spriggs, had a reputation for ruling with an iron rod. With more than 25 children in the class, aged from five to eleven and a mix of abilities, the demands on her were considerable. Miss Spriggs taught the whole school in one room, windows set high up to avoid distraction. A large bell summoned the children to school each day and Stan learned to loathe its dreary sound. Miss Spriggs used her piercing glare, staring from one group to another to ensure they all behaved. If that failed there was always the cane.

Each morning Stan walked to school with Ena Lewin, who lived with her three sisters in the house at the bottom of the lane. Being the same age and neighbours, they were also playmates. But for Stan, with his cherubic mop of curly hair, looks could be deceiving.

Each summer a mass of big juicy strawberries spread over the rector's garden. Stan watched them ripen on his way to school and began to plot how to get his hands on them. One day he lagged behind Ena and the others, feigning a sore ankle, then leapt over the wall to shove a handful of delicious berries into his mouth. Lying beneath the fruit net, he tucked in until his belly was full and stuffed a few extra ones in his pockets for good measure.

Unbeknownst to Stan, the bemused rector saw this scene unfold from his kitchen window. 'What are you up to, young man?' he asked, strolling out into the garden.

Stan peered from beneath the net, desperately trying to avoid squashing the strawberries secreted in his pockets. Seeing his hands were covered in red juice he wiped them on his trousers, forgetting his mouth was by now the colour of crimson. 'I'm trying to find my pigeons,' said Stan.

After the incident with the strawberries, Stan's growing reputation as a cheeky lad often meant he was the first to be blamed. One bright morning, Miss Spriggs was making her way to school along the main street, deep in thought, when she was struck on the head by a couple of small stones. Looking up, she spotted Stan in the distance, well within the proverbial stone's throw, and it seemed obvious who the culprit was. Despite his protests – 'I didn't do it miss, honest!' – Stan was punished and made to stand facing the wall in the corner of the classroom for the rest of the day. What Miss Spriggs failed to notice was the smirk on Stan's brother's face. It had in fact been Ken launching the missiles from the paddock, hidden behind an oak tree!

The one time Stan really did deserve a clip round the ear, he escaped any reprimand. He had sneaked out of bed under cover of darkness to climb onto the school roof. There he tied a long piece of string to the bell and hid be-

32

hind the walnut tree. He pulled hard on the string and the bell rang out in the dead of night, echoing throughout the village. Several puzzled and tired residents talked about a ghost prowling their streets but no one pointed the finger at the true transgressor.

Stan's disinterest in academia meant he failed the Eleven Plus and transferred to Melton Mowbray Secondary Modern for Boys. Although obviously bright, he found it hard to apply himself. Ernest wasn't too worried and told his boys they would learn all they needed on the farm. However, that first year, Stan came top of the class without even trying. Gradually he slipped back, only really caring for two subjects: maths and sport, which became the mainstay of his education for the next few years.

Amongst his gifts was the most amazing hand to eye coordination and he picked up most sports with ease. Whether swimming, riding, cricket or playing darts, Stan was happiest locked in competition. Aged only eleven, he applied to join the local Burrough men's cricket team. Despite his young years, they recognised a star in the making. His teacher, Mr Carter, saw how deftly this young man guided the ball around the ground and soon installed Stan as an opening batsman. Not satisfied with being pigeonholed as 'merely a batsman', Stan also offered to bowl and emerged as a complete all-rounder.

'Who's schooling you, Riley?' Mr Carter inquired one afternoon as Stan ambled back to the pavilion.

Stan nonchalantly replied, 'Nobody, sir.'

His teacher raised an eyebrow, certain such talent had to be the product of an excellent coach. 'I don't believe you, Riley!'

Stan raised his cricket bat as a mark of silent defiance and disappeared inside, quietly pleased with his efforts.

The ensuing years saw Stan play for Oakham and Sparkenhoe at Victoria Park, the former home of Leicester racecourse. Even when he was hit in the face and lost a couple of teeth, nothing could stop him winning. Word spread via the cricket grapevine and a scout came down from Yorkshire, keen to see if this young kid who had only been bowled out three times was anything more than another good village player. The spotter grabbed Stan after the innings and ushered him to a quiet corner of the club.

'£100 a match,' he said, 'at Headingley.'

It was a huge sum of money, more than Stan had ever seen in his lifetime, let alone could earn in a week. And the chance to play sport for cash was the stuff of Hollywood dreams. However, Stan knew the biggest hurdle was yet to come.

'Best ask my dad,' Stan answered.

That night, Ernest listened carefully and saw the fire in his son's eyes.

'You can go,' he said, matter of factly. Stan could hardly believe his ears. And then, 'But don't think you're ever coming back.'

Stan felt as if he'd been physically hit. Here was his big chance to make something of himself and, yet again, his father stood in his way. Why couldn't he let him go with good grace and a pat on the back?

Whatever his motivation, be it jealousy or plain parental overprotection, Ernest refused to give Stan permission to leave home. In denying the boy opportunity – as a jockey, or now as a cricketer – each refusal fostered a growing sense of resentment.

Stan yearned for a life beyond Burrough on the Hill. And he would get it, one way or another.

Perhaps as a way of rebelling against his father's Victorian attitude, Stan joined the Army Cadets to chase the action and women. By the end of 1941, the war showed no sign of ending and the village was teeming with girls from the Women's Land Army earning a shilling an hour for a fifty hour working week. A hostel was built in Somerby and they were given a month's training to learn the rudiments of farming. The women, wearing regulation brown hat, green tie and jumper, weaved their way to work on heavy men's bicycles, riding through unlit streets at the crack of dawn.

'It was a bit of shock for them,' said Bill Fryer. 'They came from the cities of Sheffield and Nottingham. Most had worked in factories and weren't used to getting up at five in the morning to milk a herd of cows.'

When Stan and Bill enlisted in the cadets they too were issued with a uniform and army boots. Both paraded up and down the main street past the church, guns by their side, but ammunition being in such short supply, they only got to try the rifle out once.

'We went up into the hills and were allowed a single shot each,' said Bill.

That may have been just as well considering the near catastrophe last time Stan held a gun. He'd been following his brother Ken up into the fields, on the lookout for a fox that was eating their mother's hens. Armed with a 12-bore hammer gun, normally fired from the shoulder, Stan liked to be prepared so his was cocked and ready to shoot.

Ken ducked under a fence and beckoned Stan to hurry up. Stan manoeuvred himself between the rails as fast as he could, but in his haste, he forgot he was carrying a gun. As he ducked, the catch snagged. To his horror, the gun fired.

Everything happened in slow motion. Stan had no time to warn Ken, all he could do was hold his breath and hope.

Seconds later, Stan opened his eyes to see a spray of shot embedded in the ground just inches away from where Ken was standing. Both boys were so badly shaken that they sat in stunned silence. It was a salutary safety lesson, one Stan never ever forgot.

The greatest challenge for Stan as a young cadet was boot camp. When he heard they were going to Bitteswell Park on the other side of the county, he contacted one of his many cousins to arrange a boys' night out, failing to appreciate cadets were barely given a moment's respite. On arrival he was ordered to yomp from Ullesthorpe Station carrying a heavy backpack and rifle.

'It was a really hot day,' said Stan. 'Three or four of the lads fainted while we were marching along, they dropped like flies and had to be picked up by an army lorry. All I wanted was to get it over with and get out on the town.'

Conditions didn't improve. By now Stan had grown into a big lad, six foot one inch in height, and bemoaned the fact he was crammed in with all his comrades. 'Each tent had at least eight cadets and we all had to sleep with our feet towards the pole in the middle. We were packed in like a tin of sardines.'

Stan decided he'd had enough and persuaded Bill they should escape under cover of darkness. Dressed in military uniform, Stan was convinced they looked old enough to impress some girls and maybe even find his cousin.

'I don't know how we managed to get back that night, what with the blackout and because we'd had a drop or two,' said Bill. He was unsure in his groggy state where they ended up, but pretty sure it wasn't with Stan's cousin.

Always one for seeking out the ladies, Stan saved up for a battered Triumph motor bike with a top speed of 60 miles per hour. Ken had ridden a bike for a couple of years, once crashing through the hedge at Somerby Police Station, and Stan listened enviously to his stories.

Given village bingo wasn't exactly a young man's idea of a great Saturday night out, the Triumph 350 came into its own at the weekend. A favourite haunt of Stan's was the Palais de Dance in Leicester, a mecca for the nimble footed during the war years.

The USA joined the war in 1941 following Japanese bombing of the Pearl Harbour naval base in Hawaii. Swathes of American troops were soon stationed in Britain in preparation for the invasion of Europe. However, Stan was not taken with the new boys in town. Not only did Stan harbour resentment against the United States' reticence to join the fight, there was another more primal reason – GI Joe was nabbing all the best-looking women.

Never was the cry 'overpaid, oversexed and over here' more keenly felt. The GIs hit back, describing their Limey hosts as 'underpaid, undersexed and under Eisenhower'. Earning over five times the wages of British servicemen and arriving laden with luxuries like Nylon stockings, chocolate and cigarettes, the Americans proved extremely attractive to the fun-starved girls in Leicester and beyond.

There was genuine concern among the military hierarchy that the British would feel undermined by the visiting Yanks. The American war department issued a pamphlet to all servicemen advising 'don't be a show off' and 'NEVER criticize the King or Queen'. They were also given a stark warning: 'The British don't know how to make a good cup of coffee.'

Stan thought the GIs were arrogant and loud. After a few beers resentment would inevitably start to bubble over. An evening out dancing wasn't always a friendly affair. Blood stains on his shirtsleeves after a dance at Twyford brought forth a barrage of questions from Stan's mother.

'Where's that from?' she demanded.

'Not me!' Stan retorted proudly.

Ernest, on the other hand, took his wartime duties much more seriously than his youngest son. Appointed village air raid warden, he marched around Burrough keen to show everyone how to use their gas masks. One resident, Mrs Smith, had great difficulty placing the mask over her face. When fastening the straps she became claustrophobic and flew into a panic. Ernest was not renowned for his patience and decided to strap the mask in place on her behalf. 'It's for your own good,' he explained, as she promptly fainted.

When peace finally came to Burrough in 1945, Stan was just entering adulthood and yet to fulfil his ambitions to leave the farm.

All that was about to change in the most dramatic of circumstances.

3

To please his dad, Stan had to show he was committed to the farm and not just out for himself. He would never have guessed in a million years that the rural art of hedge laying would heal their relationship, but somehow, once Stan decided to learn the skill, everything fell into place. As a young man, his father had been a dab hand at hedge laying and was secretly chuffed Stan had inherited his skills. Ernest suddenly had a sparkle in his eye and listened attentively to Stan at the kitchen table. They now had a common interest. In blackthorn!

Buoyed by his father's enthusiasm, Stan threw himself into action and learned everything he could. Ever the competitor, he entered a series of contests to satisfy his will to win. After a few months he was crowned All-England Hedge Laying Champion, an accolade his father never attained.

At long last, Stan felt worthy of Ernest's praise and there was the added bonus that he could now secure the farm's perimeter, country style. Mastering the ancient craft of hedge laying meant Stan could transform prickly blackthorn and holly hedgerows into sturdy boundaries. Armed with nothing more than a threatening-looking billhook – a large cutting knife – Stan got so good at working the wood that he won 28 hedge laying competitions in a row, and came second in another 'only because I was late when the car wouldn't start!'

However, Stan could be reckless in his pursuit of success. During one match he rushed the last section and accidentally grabbed a large blackthorn which penetrated deep into his middle finger. Grimacing with pain, he was rushed to Oakham Hospital.

'It was in danger of becoming so badly infected the doctor said it'd have to be amputated,' Stan said. If he lost his finger his future would be seriously compromised as he earned a living with his hands. Fortunately, a limited number of antibiotics were available and the doctor told Stan these new drugs might mean he could avoid surgery. After swallowing the first of many bullet-sized pellets, Stan's hand was cleaned, stitched and dressed to allow the healing process to begin.

Enduring a period of recuperation was sure to drive him mad. He had no patience for reading, but now found himself at a loose end and spent time flicking through the small ads. A large estate in Ireland wanted an experienced hedge layer. Stan poked his finger. It no longer made him wince. He read the ad again. It would mean leaving Cheseldyne Farm for a while and going overseas. Yet it was exactly the sort of job his father would approve of.

Stan wrote that very day to the estate owners who, impressed by his champion status, offered him a job and £15 a week – a king's ransom to Stan.

'I just had to agree to keep my wages quiet from the other workers, or they'd all want a rise,' said Stan. To clinch the deal he promised to send his dad a few bob home every week.

Two weeks later, Stan was perched on his duffle bag at Liverpool docks, waiting in the howling wind and rain to board a ship for Dublin. The Irish landowner, Mr Armitage, had told Stan to come over right away. His eager group of lads needed to be taught the finer points of hedge laying immediately. Despite Stan having no teaching experience, he accepted. 'I worked on the principal of see one, do one, teach one,' said Stan, 'and a lot of youthful bottle!'

In the October gloom, he watched the cargo being loaded as dark plumes of smoke billowed from the ship's funnels. It felt like he was journeying to the other side of the world. A shiver of apprehension ran down his spine. The inclement weather made this one of the worst months to cross the Irish Sea. For Stan, who had grown up in the landlocked Midlands, sailing was not his forte.

Climbing the gangplank, he took one look back to shore and saw the flashing lights of the Vernon Pools building on the docks and reassured himself the giant ship looked sturdy enough. Once on deck, he snapped a picture with his tiny box Brownie camera and then closed his eyes for moment allowing the dock to fade into the distance. He was on his way.

Not long into the journey, the boat started swaying sickeningly from side to side. Stan felt a rising unease and consoled himself that at least he was a strong swimmer thanks to his big brother. When they were kids, Albert pushed Stan's head under the water, the traditional way to learn to swim in the Riley household. Literally swim or sink! Stan took a huge breath and stayed under water for so long he appeared to have drowned. Albert started to panic, until his little brother broke through the surface and doggy paddled off into the distance.

Stan paced the undulating deck to try and distract himself from the fear building in his belly. It was now dark and all he could feel was his stomach lurching as the ship rocked through the violent waters. Going down below, he sought the company of fellow passengers. If nothing else, they could provide moral support.

It turned out to be a bad move. Stan lost his footing and fell the last few steps into the lounge as the boat crashed into a huge wave. Crockery shattered from the tables and scattered across the floor. People screamed as the lights flickered.

'There was a hell of a noise,' said Stan. 'It was a horrible creaking sound and I just had to get back up on deck. I didn't want to get trapped down below. It took all my strength to climb back up the stairs. When I saw emergency flares light up the night, I knew it was trouble.'

Gripping onto the railings overlooking the black sea, Stan retched, scared stiff his big adventure was destined to end before it had began. Staring into the gloom, he feared he was about to die miles away from everything and everyone he knew.

After what seemed an eternity, the captain and crew managed to guide the ship and shocked seasick passengers safely into Dublin dock. Stan ran down the gangplank, elated to be back on dry land. He decided never to tell his parents of the nightmare encountered on his maiden voyage. He didn't want to worry them. Or relive the experience.

Ahead was a long bus journey to Parkstown House, an imposing estate and country manor in southern Tipperary, just outside a village imaginatively called Horse and Jockey. It wasn't the estate hedges that grabbed Stan's imagination, rather the impressive stable block, home to a handful of handsome Irish horses. Owned for some years by the Armitage family, the current lady of the house was Marigold, daughter of wartime RAF Chief of Bomber Command, Sir Arthur 'Bomber' Harris. A few months before the end of the war, he controversially ordered the blanket fire bombing of Dresden, which killed around 25,000 civilians and reduced the city to rubble.

Marigold too was a fascinating character. It was said she had certain rituals that even her staff thought odd. On the mornings she went hunting, she would insist her butler stand to attention at the foot of the stairs with a glass of brandy in his hand. Without a word she'd remove the glass from his grasp and down it before leaving the house. And there was a tale circulating of how a lad had fallen off the top rung of a ladder onto her lounge floor. She ran over, not to check on the boy's injuries, but to see if he had damaged her parquet floor. In her spare time, her equestrian obsession was given full rein in writing novels about hunting and painting oils on canvas of her favourite horses.

Stan settled in quickly, embraced the camaraderie and slept in the stable block alongside the other labourers. They became good friends and had a great laugh, but on his first day out in the fields he thought they were pulling his leg when he asked a simple question – where do you keep the billhooks?

The troupe of trainees looked at him blankly. 'What are they?' they asked.

Stan assumed they were kidding and started searching the tool box. The men continued to shake their heads and stared at the ground. Then the truth quickly dawned.

Having travelled almost four hundred miles and risked his life to get here, Stan found himself without the tools for the job. To save face, he rushed back to his digs and dashed off a letter to his parents, requesting they post his own billhook by return. Stan wondered how he would ever live down the embarrassment.

Until the billhook arrived, he abandoned any hope of teaching and instead offered to help out in the stables. Stan would happily spend all day grooming and riding the Irish horses. It was his idea of heaven, and at the end of each day the lads tried hard to persuade him to relax with a few drinks. But Stan was never a great drinker and was soon being ribbed about how little it must take to get him drunk. He played along and tried not to appear surprised as they told story after story about a powerful local man who had been involved in a car accident. This man, it was said, knocked over and killed a poor pedestrian while inebriated. Yet the police had not followed up on the case and there was no prosecution as there were no drink-driving limits. Stan listened in disbelief.

Stan, keen to get back to the horses, would often excuse himself and the other lads gradually accepted where his heart lay. He would only open up when chatting about breeding or training. Some wondered if he'd deliberately left the billhook at home.

With the nights drawing in, Lucy May wrote back to Stan, not daring to admit how much she missed him.

Dear Stan,

We are pleased to hear you have arrived safely. Hoping this will find you well as am pleased to say this leaves us the same, except for colds. The pigs are alright, they are still dry in their huts as we have frosts. We had 3 or 4 inches of snow at the weekend, a lot of it has gone, but the lane is just like a sheet of ice. We have rung the council to come with some grit but they haven't been to this lane. Your dad took five pigs on Tuesday. They made 95 shillings, so not too bad.

I packed the bill-hook and posted it in Melton so hope you get it alright. Your Dad says you had better bank that cheque and send it straight here. Must close now as it's getting late so with love from Mam and Dad.

Hedge work did eventually come Stan's way and he spent many hours training a group of lads to lay hedges. During his spell in Ireland, he laid miles of new fencing not far from the Ballydoyle stables of celebrated trainer Vincent O'Brien. Horse racing was inevitably a regular topic of conversation. The lads were knowledgeable and Stan picked up more tips than he'd ever hoped to. It only served to make him more determined to put into practice what he learned.

The year before, he dabbled as a racing novice using some of the money saved from working at Cheseldyne Farm. He'd bought a cheap racehorse but it had not been a major success. Anything but. The intention was to ride the grandly-named Simon VIII at the Quorn Hunt. Still harbouring ambitions to be a jockey, Stan entered the traditional point-to-point, but at the last minute decided to give Simon VIII a warm-up race. He chose a woman rider for an easier debut at the Easter Monday Ladies Race in south Nottinghamshire.

Simon VIII appeared to run exceptionally well and finished a creditable fourth, but then tragedy struck. The horse collapsed and died as Stan led him back to the horse-box. As Stan constantly relived Simon VIII's sad demise, his Irish pals encouraged him to consider racing again. They sensed he had the required enthusiasm and resolve.

When the time came, Stan bid farewell to Ireland with a heavy heart. Free from the constraints of Burrough, he discovered a taste for leadership. Farming was his bread and butter, but the Irish lads had bolstered his self-belief. He left Ireland's shores with a keen sense that horse racing was a real possibility if he wanted it badly enough.

As he boarded the ship for the home journey, Stan focused on the future instead of the turbulent seas. Let's face it, he reasoned, lightning rarely strikes twice. Yet down in the cargo hold, a large consignment of cows was en-route for Liverpool. As the seas rolled, the cows herded over to one side of the ship creating a dangerous imbalance. With the ship listing at a precarious angle, the captain chose to dock across the waters in Birkenhead, rather than attempt to get the cows to spread themselves out.

'I've never been so frightened in my life,' said Stan, 'I thought this time my luck would run out and I'd be a goner. The fact it was caused by a herd of cows at sea made it more ridiculous!'

Back in Burrough there was much cause for excitement: Ernest had uncharacteristically splashed out and bought a television set, one of the first in the village. However, the new invention was not to everyone's liking. Grandma Riley, a devout Christian, thought the black box was the work of the devil and whenever the tiny television was on she would ask for her seat to be turned around to face the wall. This strange practice continued for many years until 1961 when the BBC first transmitted *Songs of Praise*. Suddenly she demanded her seat face forward and the TV be switched on without fail!

Back at work on the farm, Stan threw himself into the social scene, developing an eye for the girls and ear for jazz. Having taught himself to read music he hooked up with a band, The Anchor Boys, playing trumpet and piano accordion. Then he fell hopelessly in love. Cynthia Tiddy was a beautiful hairdresser who worked at Lewis's, one of Leicester's largest department stores. They met at a dance at Twyford Village Hall and, from that day, Cynthia never missed Stan playing in the band, watching him starry-eyed from the dance floor. Afterwards they'd speed off on his motorbike to dance the hours away at whichever village was having a do. They spent the next couple of years courting and it was assumed they would eventually marry.

Stan spent his Friday nights dressed in his best bib and tucker, driving up to her Billesdon home and escorting her out to the best place he could afford. Their amorous meetings had a way of dragging on into the wee small hours and Stan often found himself wearily weaving through the dark country lanes to get back to Burrough before dawn.

'There were at least five gates on the road from Melton,' said Stan. 'One foggy night I was on my way home at four in the morning. I must have fallen asleep and ended up in a ditch entangled with barbed wire.'

Luckily he was so relaxed he didn't do any major damage. 'I didn't break anything, but I did tear my trousers!' Stan laughed.

Around the same time his best mate, Eric Oliver, was seeing a local girl, Margaret Weston. The couples would double date, until Stan put a spanner in the works and unexpectedly split from Cynthia. He got a serious case of the jitters when her mum suggested they have a double wedding alongside Cynthia's sister. Although Stan thought Cynthia very sweet, he was not ready for married life.

'I remember Cynthia's mum coming back one evening and finding us sitting close together on the sofa,' said Stan. 'She pulled the blanket off, thinking I had my hand on her knee. I didn't – not that time anyway – but it scared me off. And then she started going on and on about the wedding.'

By way of consoling his friend, Eric voiced his own frustrations with life and admitted he wanted a bit of adventure. 'Let's join the Marines,' he said.

Stan knew he would once again have to face the wrath of Ernest. 'I'll let you know in the morning,' he stalled.

True to form, Ernest put his foot down, refusing to back his son. When Stan admitted he couldn't leave Burrough, a look of relief flashed across his friend's face. 'Can you do me a favour then?' he asked.

'Anything,' said Stan.

'Look after Margaret while I'm gone, keep an eye on her until I'm back?'

The two lads shook hands and went their separate ways. Stan kept his promise and chaperoned Margaret to the Palais de Dance and to see his band play. It wasn't long before their platonic friendship became something more serious and complicated.

Margaret was a city girl born in Braunstone with a bright mind and pretty face. She swept through the Eleven Plus and won a place at the local grammar school, but after much debate, her parents turned down the opportunity, unable to afford the school's expensive uniform. Anyway, a good education for girls was not considered essential back in the 1940s.

However, Margaret still managed to excel at school and after leaving was recruited by Ladybird Books in Loughborough, who produced 'clean and healthy' literature for children. Margaret became personal assistant to the managing director and thought she was the luckiest girl alive.

A while after Eric left for the Marines, Margaret and Stan announced they were a couple. Comfortable and happy in each other's company, they complimented one another. Margaret was the city girl and Stan the country boy.

They may have seen the world in different ways – Margaret enjoyed socialising whereas Stan preferred sport

– yet there was an undeniable spark that united them. Margaret threw herself into country life, learning to ride under Stan's tutelage on his trusty grey mare, Thunder. For five years they courted, Margaret making the journey from Loughborough on a Friday night after work to stay at Cheseldyne Farm under the watchful gaze of Lucy May and Ernest. They were both impressed with the girl who had ambition as well as spirit. Margaret, two years younger than Stan, was a modern woman with a career who, after the austerity of city life, relished the freedom and space of Burrough. Not only had she fallen in love with Stan, but also the idea of becoming a farmer's wife. Except she didn't intend to be behind the scenes, caring for children and stuck in the kitchen, she wanted to build a successful business with her future husband. Margaret saw marriage as a partnership, a meeting of equals.

First they had to find somewhere to live. The death of a neighbouring farmer meant Pasture Farm with a rent of £159 a year was vacant. A decade before, Brasenose College, Oxford, sold their 350-acre holdings in Burrough and 260 acres in Somerby and Pickwell to Ernest Cook, grandson of travel entrepreneur Thomas, for £26,000. This land was later placed in trust as part of an educational charity.

Never good with words, Stan asked Margaret to compose a letter to the Ernest Cook Trust requesting he take over Pasture Farm's tenancy. In her lunch hour at work she eagerly slipped a piece of paper into the typewriter and wrote to the trust's boss, Captain Hill of Whatley Hill and Co, in West Wycombe.

> Would you please consider my application for the tenancy of Brasenose Farm, Burrough-on-the-Hill, following the death of Mr W Black. I am 26 years of age and am at present farming with my father, Mr CE Riley. I plan to be married next spring and should very much like to make a start on my own account. I should be very pleased to give details of my financial state and references of character if my application can be considered.

Margaret took the letter to Stan for his approval. He scanned it and quickly crossed out the words 'next spring' replacing them with 'quite soon'.

Ironically, Stan's 'quite soon' was even further away than 'next spring'. Margaret had to wait another year and a half to tie the knot because Stan had another plan.

In a bid to make some cash Stan invested in a greyhound called Sandy. He loved the atmosphere of the track and the excitement of the dogs as they raced from the trap. Sandy went on to win eight in a row and came under the eagle eye of a trainer who offered Stan a straight, if highly unusual, swap: 'your greyhound for my horse.'

Stan was sorely tempted, but given the cost of training a horse compared to a greyhound, never mind his upcoming marriage, he reluctantly turned down the proposition. It was a decision he lived to regret – the horse was Polonius, a seven year-old named after Hamlet's chief advisor in

Shakespeare's infamous play. In the 1956 Grand National with jockey EF Kelly, he received a special mention for running eighteen times that season. Just like Stan's greyhound, Polonius had won eight of his previous races.

Later, Stan remembered Polonius fondly. 'I sold a tractor to a man who'd bought Polonius and won three races with him. With that news I decided to back him at 20/1 and won! I'd never seen a horse run like him before. He'd drop out of the race and be a field behind, then fly the last half mile. In one race the jockey lost his whip halfway towards the last fence and had to take his helmet off and use that instead!'

A few weeks after sending the letter, Stan gathered Margaret in his arms and spun her around. The Ernest Cook Trust had given Stan the green light on the 140-acre Pasture Farm. Stan could be his own man. A married man. 'It must have been your fancy typing,' he laughed.

Stan and Margaret married on 26 February 1955. Stan was 27 and Margaret 25. It was a freezing cold day, the snow ankle deep. Friends and family carefully made their way along the slippery path to Burrough Church, together with Margaret's bridesmaids, Joan Kemble and Sylvia Chandler. Many of the guests never arrived. The appalling conditions made roads impassable.

Harry Matthews, Stan's best man, did his best to chivvy everyone along. The bride and her attendants stepped carefully to the church in their open-toe shoes more suited to a summer's day than the depths of winter. Margaret's ivory silk dress at least had long sleeves whilst the bridesmaids shivered, arms exposed to the elements. Stan wore a three-piece wool suit and towered above everyone as he clutched onto Margaret's hand like he never intended letting her go.

Their vows complete, Stan kissed Margaret shyly. Standing in the church's portico, the sun broke through the clouds for a brief moment and the couple posed happily arm in arm for photographs. Then it was on to the Manor House for a reception, speeches and cutting of the two-tiered wedding cake. It was the perfect start to married life.

The honeymoon was another matter. A blizzard was blowing as they left the Manor. There was to be no romantic hotel or cottage by the sea. It was business as usual, with Stan scrambling out of his wedding best and into his overalls, walking across the snowy fields, laying down hay and checking on livestock. The ewes were lambing which signalled the start of a heavy workload that would push them all to the limit.

Stan sat up all night with a pregnant pig while they were still on honeymoon. The sow appeared to be in labour and Stan wanted to ensure everything went smoothly. When nothing happened, he fell asleep and awoke to find just one tiny piglet had arrived – but where were the rest? The vet later explained to a horrified Stan the pig had most probably eaten them as he slumbered. Stan immediately sold the pig onto a friend and, much to his chagrin, she produced thirteen piglets the following year – all alive and well.

It wasn't long before Pasture Farm heard the patter of tiny feet. A little over a year later, the first of three children was born, all at home; Diane in 1956, then Susan in 1958 and four years later a son, Philip, in 1962.

Now Stan was a family man. And it turned out to be much harder than he thought.

4

Christmas 1962 was one of the bleakest on record. Thick snow fell for days before the festivities began, blanketing the country in a magical white wonderland. In the Riley household, Margaret was shivering inside the freezing farmhouse with a new baby son and two lively daughters to keep occupied. Feeling isolated and alone, her days revolved around feeding the children and keeping the house warm. As she stoked the fires and dried endless washing, her situation was a world away from Ladybird Books or how she had envisaged life as a farmer's wife. A strong woman, Margaret had learned to drive a tractor, plough a field and proved her worth as an extra pair of hands dur-

ing lambing and calving. But neither she nor Stan anticipated the demands a young family would make on their
already busy lives.

Stan was working both his own and his parents' farms.
In the past few months Ernest had grown frailer and come
to rely heavily on his youngest son. As near neighbours,
Stan was conveniently on the doorstep and on call.

Ernest's other sons were putting down roots: Albert
married and moved away to nearby Hoby where, with
financial support from Ernest, he bought a farm and stables. Stan said nothing but the clear show of favouritism
stung. Ken, meanwhile, fed up with farming's unsociable
hours, became a car dealer and tarmac contractor before
successfully applying to run the local Burrough pub.

Stan had hoped he'd be free from any obligation to
work for his father once the tenancy at Pasture Farm was
secure. However, when his older brothers moved on, he
was the one left behind with the added responsibility that
came with aging parents. The family was also stunned to
discover Ernest had been diagnosed with cancer. He remained stoical as ever in the face of such news, but the
disease was debilitating and hard to control. There were
few drugs available and chemotherapy was in its infancy.
Doctors prescribed as much pain relief as they were able
but some days Ernest struggled to get out of bed, let alone
work. The freezing weather made the pain and his mood
worse.

At first, Stan figured once the heavy snow was gone everyone's spirits would improve. Nevertheless, as the days

passed there was no respite. Stan remembered the arctic winter of 1947 and the problems it brought to Burrough so soon after the war. That winter was bad enough, but this one was something else.

Each morning, Stan tuned into the BBC's *Farming Today* hopeful of good news. Instead there was a litany of doom and gloom with accounts of livestock starving to death in 20-foot drifts. Stan knew farmers would go a long way for their animals, but this was both depressing and treacherous.

He clung to the hope that Burrough had seen more than its fair share of bad weather over the years and they would get through it as they had done before, battening down the hatches and helping each other out. However, since his father's health had declined it was hard for Stan to retain his optimistic nature. At the back of his mind he couldn't shake a worrying feeling that worse was yet to come.

Over Christmas, Stan and Margaret worked hard on making the festive season as happy as they could for the two girls and their new baby brother. They lit a huge fire, cooked the turkey bought from a fellow farmer and wrapped their few presents. The white fields painted a perfect Yuletide scene.

A new year dawned with no sign of a thaw and cabin fever set in as the outside world became even less accessible. No one could deny things were really serious. January was about to unveil itself as the coldest month of the century.

Night after night temperatures plummeted way below zero, refreezing the snow into hard ice, making swathes of the country as impassable. The sea froze as far as four miles out. The chilling statistics kept on coming: temperatures fell to minus 21 degrees Celsius and 95,000 miles of road was blocked with abandoned vehicles. Even the indefatigable late night newspaper train from Manchester to Brighton arrived two days late, bringing old news of ever worsening conditions. The small hamlet of Burrough succumbed and became increasingly isolated with lanes submerged under several feet of snow. Residents now not only battled to keep warm but also find enough to eat.

By February there was still no let up. Now officially called the Big Freeze, the Grand Union Canal could no longer avoid winter's grip and froze from London to Leicester. Sporting fixtures ground to a halt the length and breadth of the country. The National Hunt season was in tatters with 94 meetings cancelled, no racing took place anywhere in England between 23 December and 7 March. Dog racing ceased when electric hares froze. It took 66 days to play out the FA Cup third round.

Each day was a fight against the bitter cold and severe disruption. Even the simplest task took an age. Stan could only be outside for a short time before his fingers and toes went numb. Growing crops was impossible.

Those farmers who managed to keep their animals warm and fed lived in fear of seeing their efforts wasted. Over 250,000 gallons of milk was thrown away because it couldn't be delivered. As the freezing days turned into weeks and then months, all attempts to dig up vegetables proved futile and these too were lost. The misery multiplied when four and a half million sheep died during what should have been a profitable lambing season. With no sign of a break in the weather, a serious food crisis loomed and prices rocketed by a third. Power cuts became a way of life while rubbish piled up with refuse collectors unable to get through. Then water pipes froze and people had to queue in the snow, shivering as they waited to get water from tankers. It was a truly miserable time. There were complaints that the country was ill equipped to deal with such treacherous conditions. Why weren't we better prepared? To alleviate the pressure, the Government called on the Royal Navy and used an icebreaker to keep key docks open.

Stan had never worked in more gruelling conditions. There were times when he wondered how he would carry on. Working one farm in this weather would be bad enough, two often seemed insurmountable. He was up before dawn and did not stop until he dropped into bed, only to do the same again the next day. Yet although he was exhausted, sleep didn't always come as the uncertainty and money worries took their toll. He had a family and a very sick parent to consider, which brought a mental weariness like no other.

Then, just when it appeared things could get no worse, tragedy struck the Riley household. During the cold spell, Ernest had become very weak. As a proud man who didn't share worries easily, little was discussed within the family. Surgery for the cancer had left an open wound which Lucy May cleaned and dressed twice a day without complaint. Married over forty years, they had been through a lot together and she saw it as her duty to do whatever she could for her husband.

Usually, at the end of each day, they sat at the table eating supper, quietly mulling over events. Tonight was no different. One moment Ernest was chatting away until he began to cough uncontrollably. Lucy May patted his back and fetched a glass of water but nothing relieved his distress. Soon, Ernest clutched at his chest and beads of sweat formed across his forehead. Lucy May ran to the phone to call Stan for help, her fingers shaking as she dialled the familiar number. By the time she got through, Ernest had lapsed into unconsciousness. All Lucy May could do now was wait for her son. And pray.

Dashing down the lane towards his parents' house, Stan slid on the ice as he tried to stay calm. It may have only taken minutes to push open the door at Cheseldyne Farm but the short distance seemed like a marathon. His mother's face told Stan everything he feared. It was too late. Ernest had passed away from a massive heart attack.

Stan told Margaret to gather the children and take them to a neighbour. Sue, their youngest daughter, was protected from the unpleasant truth and told to behave herself because Grandad was very poorly.

Helped by a neighbour, Stan carefully lifted Ernest from his chair and laid him gently on the sofa in the sitting room. He stood in stunned silence, unable to comprehend the last few minutes. He took a little comfort knowing Ernest died at home, on the farm he loved with Lucy May by his side. He was 68.

It was a dreadful time for the Rileys. Lucy May had lost her husband, the boys had lost their dad; the patriarch of the family. Life would never be the same again. In the midst of bereavement, Lucy May faced the stark truth that she would have to vacate Cheseldyne Farm and hand it back to the Ernest Cook Trust.

For Stan, now 36 and a married man with three children of his own, this was a defining moment. He had to step forward like his father would have expected.

Stan, Albert and Ken planned Ernest's funeral with Lucy May. They agreed he was to be cremated, the freezing ground unyielding for any burial. Death is a great leveller. It brings out the best and the worst in people and the Rileys were no different. When the question of money reared its ugly head at the reading of Ernest's will, the family was pushed to the limit.

Stan always assumed he would be left enough money to either invest in Pasture Farm or mortgage a farm of his own. He couldn't have been more wrong. His father had actually left him nothing. Not a bean.

Stan felt a terrible sense of rejection by the man he had looked up to and obeyed his entire life.

He may not have agreed with him, but he did as he was told. He could not see why Ernest set Albert up at Glebe Farm yet did not give or invest a penny in him. It was a bitter blow for the years of back-breaking work, dedication and so many stifled dreams. It left Stan utterly bewildered.

He didn't understand what he'd done wrong or why his father had decided to favour one child over another. Unable to find answers, he began to suffer more doubts. And, inevitably, what happened changed him. Stan felt betrayed and began to lose trust in people.

From now on he would go it alone. After a lifetime of being told what to do, Stan swore he would be guided by his gut instinct. The drive had always been there, he'd just pushed it away through fear, duty and obligation. Now the hurt and anguish freed him to make his own decisions.

To his credit, Stan's relationship with his brothers didn't suffer. He knew it wasn't Albert's fault and laid no blame at his door.

'Albert wasn't well and had bad asthma so he needed a helping hand,' Stan explained. Stan and his brothers agreed that Lucy May should move in with Albert and his wife, Sheila, at their Hoby stables. They had more room and it made sense as Sheila was a nurse and could tend to Lucy May as she got older. However, Lucy May had one condition.

'I'm not going unless my hens can go with me,' she told them.

Her sons smiled and carefully packed the precious birds into the pick up truck when the time came to move.

'What about your customers?' asked Margaret, as Lucy May was about to be driven off. 'How will they get their eggs now?'

'I'll have them ready for you,' said Lucy May without a second thought.

So from that day on, every week without fail, Margaret jumped in the car and drove to her brother-in-law's to collect freshly laid eggs and sold them back in Burrough. Margaret never dare ask why Lucy May didn't want to sell her eggs in Hoby; she just did as she was told.

With Ernest gone, it was crystal clear that Stan was now the boss. His strict father had undoubtedly seen something in Stan that reminded him of his younger self. There was a steel about Stan, he was a survivor. Maybe that's why, in the end, Ernest let his youngest son fend for himself.

However, Stan couldn't shake off the disappointment and it made mourning his father difficult. Over the subsequent months he became withdrawn, placing a great strain on his marriage with Margaret. He shut himself away, shunning family and friends.

These dark times gave him long periods to think. At first it was only a germ of an idea, but it grew quickly. He decided that, without his father around, he didn't want to be restricted to farming and he wanted to make a living from something more exciting.

A month after Ernest's death, Dr Richard Beeching, a former businessman with ICI, published his long-awaited report on the state of the nation's railways. Britain had more railway track than the USA, much of it unprofitable with too few passengers and an unwieldy labour force. Dr Beeching was earmarked as the man to transform the rail network back into the black and received the very handsome fee of £24,000 a year to get the job done. It was a controversially high wage, almost double Prime Minister Harold Macmillan's salary.

Beeching's task was to identify where the railway could make savings and implement the appropriate cuts. Following a rise in the numbers of cars and roads, investment in the rail network was being reduced as it was haemorrhaging money, a staggering £140 million a year.

Beeching did not have an easy ride. Although the railway network was nationalised in 1948, thousands of miles of track had already closed and his new proposals threatened to isolate rural communities, leaving them without any form of public transport.

On 27 March 1963, Beeching recommended a further 6,000 miles of lines, mostly in the countryside, be closed. Over two thousand stations were to go with 70,000 job losses. The Government welcomed the report but history was not so kind. Beeching later defended his actions, saying, 'I suppose I'll always be looked upon as the axe man, but it was surgery, not mad chopping.'

For good or bad, Beeching changed the face of Britain. And Stan spotted a chance to make money.

He heard whispers that John O'Gaunt station was about to be sold off. Sorely tempted to buy it, he was nevertheless unsure about property development as his first big venture. When £7,000 (equivalent to £124,000 today) was touted for three run-down cottages and the station, he pulled out. He just couldn't get that kind of money together, especially when further investment would be needed to renovate and develop the buildings before he could sell them on.

But as a result of these discussions, Stan had his ear to the ground and learned something to his advantage. The closure of the track meant scrap metal merchants were buying up the disused rails, leaving miles and miles of unused and perfectly serviceable oak sleepers beneath. It was a golden opportunity. He had to act fast.

Stan brushed down his best suit, polished his shoes and went to see the bank manager. He had no intention of leaving the meeting without a deal. And this time, he'd done his homework.

The manager, impressed by Stan's careful calculations, his eye for a business opportunity and straightforward plan to make a profit, did not hesitate. Within an hour, Stan had a new career: as a timber merchant.

He had done it. Alone.

5

A few miles down the road from Stan, John Kennelly, a former jockey who was famously pipped at the post in the 1964 Grand National on Purple Silk, had spent £100 buying a section of Dr Beeching's unwanted railway line. Now a trainer working out of Oakham, he was looking to expand his business and wanted to train horses all year round.

Once stripped of the track and sleepers, he figured the old line would make the perfect gallops. It was straight, private and well protected from the elements by high steep banks. He invested a further £2000 and got to work.

Stan heard of John's plan and considered it a brilliant idea. If only he'd thought of it first. However, he had his own investment and although buying and selling sleepers wasn't as glamorous as Kennelly's notion, it did have sustainability.

Something as simple as buying and selling wood was going to change Stan's way of life. All he had to do was keep a cool head and turn a profit. Having spotted a gap in the market, he put his money where his mouth was, spurred on by a new found determination to make a success of himself. One thing remained the same: he was going to do most of the hard work himself. Each oak sleeper weighed a back-breaking 100 kilograms and had to be manhandled from the side of the track to Stan's newly acquired shed, which he proudly called a timber yard, at John O'Gaunt station. From there they were sorted and stacked, ready to be sold on to waiting customers. Or, for a modest fee, Stan provided a delivery service and would drop the sleepers off from a small but serviceable truck proudly inscribed with the Riley logo.

The demand was immediate and insatiable. Customers wanted sleepers to create raised beds for vegetable patches or retaining walls. Others had plans for paths, steps and patios. Some used them for general building work. Adaptable, durable and weighty, there was no wastage with the wood, even rotten sleepers could be chopped up and sold for kindling. Stan's sleepers were eventually dispersed to all four corners of Leicestershire and beyond. On the busiest of days, he couldn't quite believe his luck.

Most of his payments came in hard cash – American Express had just been introduced and only the wealthy had credit cards. Rather than leave a pile of pound notes unguarded in the till at his timber yard, Stan took the whole lot back home at night then agonised over where to put it. During some renovation work he discovered a loose brick in a stable wall. Rather than cement it back in place, he decided it would make the perfect hiding place for the day's takings. He slept more soundly knowing he was the only one who knew where the roll of cash was concealed, and the following day he would deposit the small bundle at the bank. Each time it felt like he had struck gold.

As turnover increased, the whole family got involved. Youngest daughter Sue, not yet ten years old, would obediently answer the telephone reading from a script carefully prepared by her dad. Beginning with a very grown up, 'Hello Somerby 304,' she'd politely ask for the caller's number and in her best voice inform them, 'Mr Riley will call you back shortly.' No sooner had the receiver been replaced, Sue would dash outside to find her dad and let him know another order was waiting. No matter what the time of day, he was more than happy to oblige.

As word spread, Stan sensed his new business was absolutely the right move. 'I never had any doubt,' he said. Demand went through the roof. 'I had them queuing up outside the yard with their trailers and tractors.'

Business was so brisk it wasn't long before more help was needed and Stan approached Angela Thorpe, a local girl, known for being good with numbers. She was quite shocked seeing Stan striding up the pathway with a bunch of spreadsheets in his hand. 'He arrived out of the blue asking if I'd do some bookkeeping for him.'

At first she was a little reserved. The Rileys were a big family and they could be more than a little intimidating.

'I remember Stan's mum,' said Angela. 'When we were kids the Rileys had some apple trees and us village kids helped ourselves scrumping. One day she caught us and said, "Anytime you want an apple just you ask." So next time we went and knocked on the door and said, "Mrs Riley, can we please have an apple?" and she said, "No you can't!" '

Angela, young and looking for work, quickly overcame her reticence and accepted Stan's offer. Local employment was hard to reject, even when it turned out to be a bit basic. 'There was no typewriter, so everything had to be handwritten, which obviously took a while.' Angela was nevertheless grateful.

Provided she did the work, Angela was left to her own devices and worked hours that suited her. 'Stan came round once a month,' she said, 'and pointed out who needed a bill and who needed a reminder.' Pretty soon they had an efficient streamlined system in place. Things at Pasture Farm were not as straightforward. With more money in the family pot, Margaret was convinced they could now afford to replace a few items around the house. The furniture she'd bought with her own savings was tired and worn. She'd had enough of the wartime creed 'make do and mend'. Now business was on the up, she wanted to put the last ten years behind them.

They had few luxuries: Margaret still cooked on a basic electric stove and washed clothes in an old twin tub. Pasture Farm had no central heating, just two coal fires, and the electric heaters were only allowed on when there was snow on the ground. After a long day helping on the farm or checking over the books, Margaret's evenings were spent making clothes for the children as well as patching up her own. She felt the time had come for a few home comforts, a little indulgence to reward the hard work.

Yet whenever she pressed Stan about replacing the washing machine for something a little more reliable his response was always the same. 'We can't afford it yet.'

Margaret knew differently. In charge of credit control, she was well aware of what was going on in the timber yard – the sleepers were selling well and profitably. Possessing a good head for figures, she saw week on week exactly how much money was made. Given the upturn in their family's fortunes she certainly didn't think it unreasonable to increase the housekeeping.

Stan wouldn't budge. His requirements were basic and, having made some money, he didn't want it frittered away on what he considered to be extravagances. His reasoning never changed: they lived in a pretty village surrounded by open countryside where the kids could play and had animals to care for, they never went hungry; they were their own boss. He knew what it meant to be poor and didn't want to go there again. Any money they made should be tucked away for a rainy day or reinvested in the business.

The more Margaret pushed, the more Stan held fast and, ever a man of few words, refused to discuss it further. Margaret tried everything: she even stopped doing his laundry in protest, only to be further infuriated when Stan bought new shirts rather than wash his dirty ones.

The cracks in their relationship grew deep and there were frequent rows followed by stony silences. They led increasingly separate lives despite living under one roof. It got so bad Margaret couldn't see any alternative but to leave and found a cottage to rent in nearby Somerby. With no one to turn to, she confided in her brother, Geoffrey, who promised to decorate her new home ready for when she and the children moved in. But at the very last minute Margaret had a change of heart, worn down and afraid of how she would make a living on her own. If she was frozen out of Stan's new business, her situation would become even more difficult. So she let the cottage, and chance of a new life, go.

In an attempt to mend the fractured relationship rather than give up on the marriage, she grasped hold of what had brought her and Stan together in the first place. 'She had a dream about how it was meant to be and kept trying to make it work,' said their daughter, Sue.

But try as they might, Stan and Margaret had both changed and things were never the same again. For light relief, Stan turned his attention back to his first love: horses. He'd always kept a couple of mares on the farm, still enjoyed riding and he made sure the children were raised around ponies. One character, Marco Polo, was always so full of beans that he had to be galloped around the field for a good half hour to sap him of energy before there was any chance of getting in the saddle.

And there was a sweet-looking Shetland pony, Merry Legs, the complete opposite of Marco Polo, at her happiest standing still. 'You could light a bonfire under Merry Legs and she wouldn't move,' said Stan. The one thing that got her going was the sight of other horses. And then you couldn't stop her. 'At one meet she went ballistic, got frisky and raced a Barton's bus down Burrough Main Street!'

Now in his forties, all dreams of becoming a jockey gone, Stan thought he would try his hand at training and applied for a permit from the Jockey Club. It gave him a legitimate reason to spend time away from home, plus he could now train and enter horses in whatever races he liked. However, the rules dictated he had just three seasons to prove himself with a winner otherwise he would be stripped of the licence.

Wasting no time, Stan bought a horse called Happy Jack to go alongside another recent acquisition, Sue's Harmony. Neither of them was ready to set the world alight but he was hopeful they would improve under his tutelage.

There was one important task remaining: Stan needed to design his official riding silks. Sifting through old balls of wool tucked away at the back of the dresser drawer, he found a rainbow of shades, oddments left over from various jumpers, scarves and cushions. Stan wanted something that would really stand out so he chose a striking palette of orange, black and kingfisher blue. Sketching out a design on the back of an envelope, he decided it looked pretty smart. Now he had to track down someone skilled enough to turn his drawing into an actual garment. Stan racked his brain for somebody who was a dab hand with knitting needles. Of course! He thought of his old school pal, Ena Lewin, the little girl down the road who walked to school with him when they were only five years old. She had long moved on and married a local farmer, Bill Fryer, but was living nearby at Grange Farm in Somerby. The timing was perfect. Bill said, 'Ena's sister, Vera, bought a knitting machine so she could make a few extra bob. The trouble was she had no idea how to make it work. So Ena took it off her hands and went to classes. She made loads of stuff for the children, which they only wore under duress! Then Stan asked if she could help make the top for his silks.'

Not exactly au fait with knitting patterns, Stan forgot to tell Ena the exact width of each black and orange hoop to go around a rider's arms. Jockey Club rules clearly state they must be a specific circumference. In his haste to get the job done, Stan left out this small but vital detail.

'The hoops ended up being too wide,' said Bill, 'and Ena had to unpick it all. There was some strong language that day, I can tell you!'

Ena had to start all over again and worked late into the night to get it exactly right. There was just enough wool to finish the job.

However, it wasn't the jockey's silks that got Happy Jack noticed. A large beast, he had a strangely saggy back which delighted Stan's children. They weren't too bothered if he won but they were mesmerised by his unusual physique. Soon they were making up funny little songs about Jack: 'Happy Jack was a hack/With a dip in his back.'

The whole family laughed each time the ditty was recited. Unfortunately, jockeys didn't find him quite so amusing. Anything but. They were scared witless by his unpredictability and several refused to ride him at all. Happy Jack was soon dubbed The Killer.

'He'd run a few times but never managed to complete the course, always falling at the ditch. It got so bad I couldn't get a ride for him,' said Stan. 'Then I found a jockey who reckoned he could ride anything. He managed to do one circuit, then pulled up scared and refused to go any further. It proved to me that if The Killer didn't want to jump, nobody could make him!'

Sue thought of Happy Jack with rather more affection. 'He was a lovely horse, with a lovely temperament,' she said, 'but then I was never concerned if he won, or not. And that was Dad's prime objective. Without a win, he'd be the loser.'

By the start of the 1970s, Stan had built a reputation for his no-nonsense approach to business. He had a good nose for a deal and kept constantly busy, preferring to work rather than confront the emotional maelstrom at home. Things were ticking over nicely at the timber yard and his horses were a fun diversion, yet Stan was restless.

When he got a call from his mate Ernie Palfreyman in Somersby, Stan listened hard. Ernie had heard about a horse called Green Monkey up for auction at Leicester Market. It was definitely worthwhile Stan making a bid, Ernie insisted, Green Monkey was from good breeding stock even though she was in poor shape, mainly due to problems with her present owner. Some old boy was supposed to be feeding her but when the weather turned he had been unable to leave his house and get to the poor mare in the field.

Stan was intrigued. It turned out Green Monkey's good breeding was no secret and several people had expressed an interest in buying her. On the day of the sale, Stan set off early, eager to get there before the crowds. He had a funny feeling about this one.

Wasting no time, he looked her over. She was indeed in a sorry state, painfully thin, undernourished and showing signs of ringworm. A vet appeared interested at first, but after a more thorough examination decided she would require too much work to get back to full health. Then a succession of potential buyers arrived, none of them staying too long. When the auction started a few hands shot into the air, while Stan watched from the back and kept his cool. Eventually, interest ground to a halt at £450.

Only then did Stan place a bid. As the gavel fell for the final time, Stan became Green Monkey's new owner.

'I believed in her the first time I saw her,' said Stan. 'I knew the reason she was looking so bad was simply that she hadn't been properly fed, there was nothing else wrong. In my eyes, every penny was money well spent.'

Many doubted his judgement, including the rest of the Riley family. The next day a horsebox drove into Burrough and parked up at the end of King's Lane with two horses inside. Sue ran outside with her dad, eager to greet the new arrival. Stan nodded at the driver – his neighbour, Mr Pegge, who owned a large livery yard in Somerby and had offered to transport Green Monkey back to Burrough along with a horse he too had bought at the sales. A magnificent beast trundled down the gangway into the lane and Sue bristled with delight. 'It was a fantastic looking horse, with a lovely coat,' she remembers, smiling from ear to ear.

Seconds later a sad creature, all skin and bones, popped its head out. It had a tatty coat and forlorn look on its tired face. This horse had to be coaxed with a fair amount of bran mash until it stepped gingerly from the box and stood very still and quiet as the beautiful horse was led back inside.

Sue's mouth fell open. 'Dad! Dad! They've given us the wrong horse!' she cried, pointing at the exhausted heap before them.

Stan glanced at his daughter's distraught face and shook his head. 'Don't you worry, love,' he said. 'She'll be alright, she's with us now.'

Ignoring comments from passers by, Stan slowly led Green Monkey to the paddock behind the church. Hungry and weak, she slowly grazed on the grass and settled down in her new environment.

Stan admitted, 'I got a bargain but I was ashamed to lead her through the village. She was in such a state, she could barely stand up.' He watched Green Monkey for a moment then went inside and called the blacksmith to come and trim her overgrown hooves. Stan examined her scruffy, patchy coat, especially along her neck where the true extent of the ringworm quickly became apparent. He applied antiseptic scrub and rinsed it off with vinegary water to stop the fungi from growing back.

As for the vet, Stan had already heard his opinion, so didn't bother contacting him. One look at Green Monkey in the rich pasture and Stan knew she was going to thrive, even if the next few weeks would prove to be a labour of love. Slowly, Green Monkey gained weight, her spirits improved and she relaxed in her new home. There was no secret to her recovery, just good food, plenty of attention and a warm bed. She stayed out in the paddock all day and was brought into her stable – reluctantly – at night. She'd have a haynet every evening and a nutritious breakfast in the morning before going out again. Stan was meticulous about the mix, alternating between a bowl of prepared horse pellets spooned from the feed supplier's sacks and a homemade bran mash, a combination of bran and oats mixed together with hot water and left to cool. Green Monkey loved to eat the bran mash when it was still slightly warm, especially when a few extra carrot chunks were thrown on top. Although some owners swore a healthy horse needed a mixture of stout and bran mash, Stan never believed it. He provided an alcohol-free diet – there was to be no beer and no apples on his menu!

During the summer months, Green Monkey was turned out into a much larger field, about a mile away from the village. She seemed happy here and took a great deal of persuading to leave the space and freedom of the bigger paddock. Despite her protestations, every evening she was brought back to the safety of the yard and stabled. Green Monkey always made it plain she much preferred to stay out in open spaces. One evening Stan popped out to check on her and discovered the stable door wide open with Green Monkey nowhere to be seen.

'I panicked a bit and thought she'd been stolen,' he said. 'Then I decided to go and check her field because I always had a job getting her to come in at all.'

Sure enough, Green Monkey was half a mile away standing patiently by the field gate, waiting to be let inside.

'I brought her back and spent the next hour replacing the door latch on her stable to make sure she couldn't get out again,' said Stan.

After that she became known as Cheeky Monkey. If she was clever enough to undo a door latch, walk herself through the village and along the track to her favourite place, there must be something special about her.

She was a lovely horse with a great temperament so Stan had no hesitation about lavishing her with kindness, patience and a good diet.

'She took six months to build up because she'd been so neglected,' said Stan. 'But she was worth every moment as she had a sweet nature.'

Once in better health, Green Monkey was more than happy to be ridden. Each morning Stan took her out for 45 minutes without fail. First he tried a steady walking pace, gradually increasing her speed to a canter, and after a few weeks when she was going particularly well, Stan set up hurdles in a field at the bottom of Burrough Hill. Word spread around the village that Green Monkey was not only a lovely animal but a really good ride. Neighbours looked on admiringly at how fit and well she had become. Offers soon poured in to ride her whenever Stan was busy. He gratefully accepted and twice a week neighbours would take Green Monkey from the yard and ride her around the vales of Burrough on the Hill.

Surprisingly, this ad hoc training did her racing no harm either. She became a respectable competitor and managed fourth place out of 27 starters in a hurdle race at Ludlow. Not bad for a horse once considered on the brink of death.

It made Stan think what would happen if he further invested in Green Monkey.

'I watched Monkey when she was well and fit and thought what a picture she looked, and then I asked myself, what the hell am I doing with such a beautiful horse? She should be with a top trainer, not me.'

For Stan's wife, Margaret, the arrival of Green Monkey was all too much. The more love and affection he poured on his horse, the more she felt neglected. It was like she'd been replaced.

'I could hear them arguing at the top of the stairs,' said Sue. 'Mum was complaining, "The more I do, the more you make me do!" They were complete opposites. He was a farmer and she was a townie and their parenting skills clashed because they came from such different backgrounds. Mum was well educated despite missing out on grammar school. She managed to become head girl and she'd always be pushing us. It was "do your homework" and "education, education" because she didn't get her chance. Dad wasn't really an educated person, although he was anything but unintelligent. He just didn't value it in the same way. I think because he's old fashioned, he assumed girls would get married and have kids. So what was the point?'

Unable to stand the tension and rows any longer, Margaret decided to finally take control of her life. She'd done her best and given of herself to make the marriage work, but it didn't work. The fairytale of being a farmer's wife was far from her reality. It was hard, gruelling work, which for Margaret brought few rewards. Quietly, she planned leaving again, this time for good. After finding a job, she rented a small cottage close by and sadly announced the marriage was at an end. The children were eight, eleven and thirteen.

'Both my parents were strong characters,' Sue said, 'and I can see how Mum had had enough.'

As always in such matters, there were complications. Diane, the oldest child and now a teenager, adored riding. It was her passion. She certainly didn't want to be separated from the horses and refused point blank to go with her mother to their new house.

Margaret assumed Diane would change her mind once she'd got used to the shock of the separation. She hoped it was only a matter of time before Diane followed. However, Diane remained resolute even after her mum had left Pasture Farm with Sue and Philip and moved into a cottage. Margaret decided maybe Diana needed a cooling off period and backed off for a while.

Sue always had a soft spot for her dad, and wanted regular contact. Once a week she'd cycle over and spend the day at the farm. It looked for a little while like some form of normality was returning to the Riley family, albeit in separate households.

After her days with Stan, Sue would go home and relate all she had seen and done to her mum. 'Guess what? Dad's bought a new sofa.' And another time, 'Dad's bought a new table.'

It was fuel to a flame. After all the years of scrimping and saving, Margaret saw red. Why was he spending money as soon as she had gone? She couldn't understand and struggled to keep her feelings from the children.

Stan meanwhile, came down to earth with a bump, quickly realizing just how much Margaret had done at home and in the business. Her departure was a huge loss. He could barely cope with work and taking care of Diane, let alone Sue and Philip when they came to stay. Eventually he did the most practical thing, with no thought to how Margaret might react, or what the consequences could be for Diane – Stan advertised for a live-in housekeeper. To attract the right person, he tidied the place up a bit, bought a few things and replaced the furniture Margaret had taken to the cottage.

It didn't take long to find someone. From the moment he sat down and chatted to Kathleen Ward, a warm, straightforward woman who had been through her own marriage breakdown and was looking for a fresh start, Stan knew she was right for the job. Kath moved in soon after. Then the trouble and the gossip really started.

Burrough is a small village and it was hard to keep a secret from the neighbours. It was also very easy to get the wrong end of the stick. With a new woman in residence at Pasture Farm, it wasn't long before Margaret heard – and believed – the rumours.

Sue, in one of her post-visit chats, mentioned the 'new lady' living with Dad and how nice she was. Margaret was fuming. It wasn't enough that Stan had renewed his furniture, he'd replaced her as well. After hearing about

Stan's new housekeeper and their supposed relationship, Margaret reacted completely out of character.

'Mum was absolutely furious with me,' said Sue. 'She just said, "Right, if you like her that much, you can go and live there!" It was terrible. In retrospect, I think she was just point-scoring, but it was terrible.'

Margaret packed Sue a suitcase and drove her to Pasture Farm.

'It was awful,' said Sue. 'I was so confused. I knocked on the door but no one was there and I kept wondering if maybe I could stay with the next-door neighbour.'

When Stan didn't answer, Margaret took Sue back to the cottage and she hoped everything would blow over by morning. However, next day Margaret still hadn't calmed down and true to her word, returned again to Pasture Farm.

'I think she reckoned by sending me to Dad's, she'd put the cat among the pigeons,' said Sue. 'She knew me and Diane would clash and hoped I'd come back and behave myself. But to be honest, I got on very well with Kath. She was lovely to me. She took me clothes shopping and bought me proper pants from the Co-op so I wouldn't have to wear homemade ones, like when I was with Mum. I never thought at the time that was because Dad kept Mum short of money.'

Sue soon settled back in with her dad enjoying a slightly more affluent lifestyle. After a couple of months, she showed no signs of wanting to move back to her mum.

Once Margaret realised Sue was not coming home, she deeply regretted what had happened. It had been done in a fit of pique when she was beside herself with anger. By now though, relations with Stan were at an all-time low. Feeling unable to discuss the children with him, Margaret started legal proceedings to get her daughter back.

'I had to go to official chambers in Melton Mowbray,' said Sue. 'A judge simply asked me, "Who do you want to live with?" and I was told, "Forget that your dad and Kath are here. Your mum wants you to live with her, but you can choose." '

Sue replied without hesitation, 'Dad and Kath.' Three words that changed everything.

It took many years before Margaret confessed her devastation to her daughter about the judgement. It hadn't been what she expected and she suffered terrible guilt at the outcome. Sadly, it also made trusting each other very difficult.

Sue visited her mum once a week. 'I'd go each Wednesday on the way back from school. I'd mow her lawn then get the next bus home. I felt a bit of resentment for a while.'

Meanwhile, things weren't going at all well between Diane and Kath. Stan's laissez-faire attitude towards his oldest daughter made for interesting times. 'Diane was going through that stage where she wanted to paint the walls black. And Dad, being Dad, let her,' said Sue. 'But they had dreadful arguments about Kath. If Kath was upset, then Dad was upset. Then Diane began sleeping in a caravan in the yard.'

Shortly afterwards Diane enrolled on a beauty therapist course at college and left home. Philip remained in the cottage with his mum and eventually adopted Margaret's maiden name, Weston, to that of Riley – a mark of where his loyalties lay.

Margaret and Stan divorced and eventually tried to get on with their lives.

For Stan, that meant one thing: he was free to devote his life to becoming a horse breeder.

6

In a small village, the closure of the post office is big news. Before coffee culture, it was the place to meet, chat and do business. So when rumours started that Burrough was to lose a major part of its community, there was fighting talk.

These were tense times. The miners were on strike for the first time since 1926, leading Prime Minister Edward Heath to declare a state of emergency and a three-day working week to save electricity. Still there were power cuts and regular blackouts as three-quarters of the country's electricity came from coal-burning power stations. By 1972, unemployment rose to over one million.

And while the loss of a post office may not have made national news, the villagers of Burrough felt the effects of the economic crisis and tried to protect the fabric of their lives. Stan sensed the villagers' growing unease.

Now in his mid-forties, Stan found farming more of a physical challenge. Coping with the day-to-day demands of livestock and crops didn't appeal in the same way as the early days. Although he'd diversified into timber, his stock of sleepers was dwindling and unlikely to last much longer. Dabbling in horse training had also so far failed to set his world alight. There was no sign of a winning horse in his small stable and he had less than twelve months to run on his licence.

He had to act fast and think long term.

He'd had his eye on a particular property in Burrough for years. Brasenose House was opposite Pasture Farm and he used to send Diane, Sue and Philip there to buy sweets. The previous owners set up a table inside the front door and villagers would choose what they wanted from a limited range of essentials and confectionary. If no one was around to take the money, you'd leave an IOU note and settle the bill later. It was the simplest of convenience stores right on the doorstep, avoiding a journey into Somerby. People trusted each other to use the honesty system and it worked well. It may not have been that profitable for the proprietor, but it cultivated a community feeling. However, all good things must end and the owners moved on, taking their confectionary table with them. Brasenose House stood empty, unloved and unwanted.

For Stan, it sparked an idea. He wanted somewhere better for him and Kath and this looked like the ideal place.

Their relationship was flourishing. What began as an acquaintance through work blossomed into friendship, then love. Soon Stan couldn't live without Kath. She was his anchor and inner strength. Stan made Kath smile with his 'can do' attitude to life, and although he found it hard to express emotion, he always took care of her. Their relationship was based on mutual respect and a cast-iron agreement never to get married. They had both been there before, it hadn't worked out and neither wanted to tempt fate again. Besides, they didn't need a piece of paper to say they were a team.

Recently though, despite being seven years younger than Stan, Kath was feeling constantly tired, the sort of bone-crushing exhaustion that can't be fixed by a few early nights. Never one to complain, she carried on helping around the farm and with the horses. During her down time she'd earn a bit of extra cash doing overlocking piece work. Sewing relaxed her, she could lose herself making soft furnishings and altering clothes. It was therapeutic.

For the last few weeks, however, whenever she walked upstairs, Kath felt a little out of breath and a bit light-headed. She assumed she was overdoing things and burning the candle at both ends, but thought things would get better on their own and soldiered on. One day, a niggling pain in her chest refused to budge. She took a couple of indigestion tablets and sipped on peppermint tea. Carrying about her normal business she tried to work it off, until she felt nauseous and broke out in a clammy sweat.

Stan found her flat out on the sofa, looking grey with pain. She said it felt like an elephant was sitting on her chest. Stan immediately called an ambulance.

The medics arrived and rushed her to hospital. Her life was in the balance. Suddenly everyone had to come to terms with the fact that, at just 39 years old, Kath had suffered a major heart attack. Stan swore if Kath survived, things would change. He would no longer farm. Instead, they would pursue a new business venture, something they'd talked about for a long time: he and Kath would become postmaster and mistress, running a local post office-cum-shop. It was their second chance.

Once out of intensive care, Kath gradually improved. When Stan told her of his idea, she couldn't have been more delighted. The heart attack had been a warning for sure, but she wanted to move on. Never the kind of woman to give in easily, living half a life wasn't Kath's way.

Leaving agriculture would mean losing Pasture Farm, but what better place to live and work than Brasenose House? Together they would put the soul back into Burrough. Mindful of how much Kath could take on, Stan still reckoned he could clinch a deal. He had to.

First was the small issue of buying Brasenose House, on the market for £4,000, far beyond Stan's means if he wanted to make alterations and start a new business. 'It was a sandstone three-storey house that was virtually derelict,' he said. 'After a few calculations I offered £1,700 – less than half the asking price, then I sat back and waited.'

He planned to use the time carefully and went out on a limb to broker a deal with his landlord, the Ernest Cook Trust. They were keen to get back Pasture Farm and all its land. However, there was a major problem with ending his tenancy – Stan needed stables for his horses. He couldn't afford to buy Brasenose and rent out new premises for his animals. Ironically, the difficult economic situation worked in Stan's favour. With a recession looming, there wasn't a lot of spare cash around and Stan's offer came at a time when people were feeling a growing sense of desperation. 'You couldn't sell places very easily in those days,' said Stan. 'They nearly snatched my hand off.'

So with Brasenose House in the bag, Stan was finally on the property ladder. Out of adversity came a brand new start and he was a proud property owner. 'Dad was great at spotting a niche, and just going for it,' said Sue.

But how would Stan continue to care for his horses? Where would they graze? And where would he train them?

Stan set up a further meeting with the Ernest Cook Trust. His opening gambit centred on vacating Pasture Farm. It was a run down sprawling property ideal for someone prepared to spend time and money converting it into a modern home.

He offered to relinquish the tenancy and almost 150 acres of land. There was one make or break condition: in exchange he must be given ownership of the stables a little further down the lane. This was real brinkmanship.

Perhaps a less confident individual would have offered to lease the stables, but Stan felt the Riley family had worked hard for the trust. On the assumption 'you don't get if you don't ask', he went for it. It didn't take long for the Ernest Cook Trust to respond. They gracefully agreed Stan deserved something for his years of loyal service and regular payments. Pasture Farm was a valuable asset and the land had appreciated over time, so a couple of tired-looking stables were a fair exchange. It didn't take long for the necessary paperwork to be drawn up.

Suddenly it dawned on Stan that for the first time in his life, he didn't have any land. It felt strange, as if part of him was missing. And on a practical level he still needed somewhere for his horses. He figured out a solution. Many of his Burrough neighbours were landowners and Stan put the word out that he was looking to lease a small meadow. After only a few days he found the ideal spot with a lush paddock so the horses – and Stan – were finally happy.

The restoration of Brasenose House wasn't quite as straightforward. He had to make the building habitable very quickly so they could move in. He worked long hours, redecorating every room to get the place ready. With each emulsioned wall, Stan took another step towards his future.

'Kath thought she was going to live in Spain!' Stan joked. 'Everywhere was painted white.'

Meanwhile Kath was busy learning the rudimentaries of how to manage a post office. There were courses to attend and endless regulations and procedures to read, which turned out to be a great distraction from her heart problems. Although she still tired easily and took an array of tablets, these were exciting times. Even if she felt weak, she never said a word so as not to alarm anyone, especially Stan.

'She never ever complained,' said Sue. 'Not once. She just smiled and got on with it. I'd see her taking various pills for this and that, including Warfarin, a blood thinner, but she never made her health an issue.'

The conversion of Brasenose House, though basic, was swift. Stan couldn't afford professional shop fitters but he had to make the property work as a home as well as a business. Using his own skills and labour, he created a shop and post office in the downstairs front room.

'You went up the steps, through the door, turn right for the post office,' said Stan. 'The rest of the house was private.'

There was a freezer for ice cream, a card stand, a counter with sweets and all the necessary Royal Mail paraphernalia. They sold tinned soups, eggs and cheese, gradually increasing the stock to satisfy demand. And when villagers asked about a home delivery service, Stan was more than happy to oblige.

Business was brisk from day one. It was good to have a shop as a focus for the community again and villagers showed their gratitude by becoming regular customers. Kath relished the daily contact with people. But one thing proved a little tiresome; visitors and day trippers alike all asked the same question: 'Ay up me duck. Where can we get a cuppa and some cake?'

Burrough had become a popular destination for tourists keen to visit the old Iron Age hill fort that towered 700 feet above the village. Its breathtaking panoramic views over glorious countryside promised a lovely outing on a sunny day.

During the Middle Ages, the village was a centre for shooting, wrestling and dancing, with an annual mini-Olympic games every Whit Monday. Archaeologists and historians weren't the only ones interested in the area, and by 1970 Leicestershire County Council spotted its potential and were leasing land from the Ernest Cook Trust, promoting it as an area of outstanding natural beauty. Although it was enjoyed by ramblers, families and historians, the local facilities were incredibly meagre and on Sundays non-existent.

'There was nowhere for tourists to eat,' said Stan. 'We were getting all these customers asking about a tearoom, so I thought we may as well open one.'

Kath wanted to start small and build gradually. It was important they kept control because with the pre-existing shop and post office, the business was about to become a seven-day operation.

Angela, who had helped with Stan's bookkeeping at the timber yard some years before, remembers the day he turned up with yet another job offer. 'He came round and asked if I wanted to work in the post office, do a few hours for them. I was a young mum and it was the perfect arrangement. They agreed to let me take my daughter, Julie, with me. She was only a year old and used to sit on Stan's knee. She loved him. Stan and Kath were just fantastic.'

The working conditions however, took some getting used to. Stan had bought old stock because it was all he could afford.

'The post office had one long counter and the most ancient till I'd ever seen,' said Angela. 'I used to have to put the figures in and pull a handle, there was nothing electronic. I had an old cheese wire on the counter that kept snapping, and a big tin of biscuits that I had to weigh out using post office scales. If there were a lot of people in the shop they had to wait and I had to get on with it. Kath might be in the back and I'd shout her to come through if it got really busy.'

As trade picked up, the shop expanded its range, though not everyone was au fait with the eclectic mix of products.

'Stan decided to stock some Durex and put them on the shelves,' said Angela. 'For that to be in a little village shop really wasn't the done thing! An old lady came in one day and said, "I need some shampoo me duck," and went over and picked a packet of Durex and asked, "Do these lather up well?" Stan burst out laughing and I had to keep a straight face. I thought how do I explain it? I said, "The gentlemen use that one," and she put it back.'

Kath, meanwhile, was spending more time in the kitchen working on her best scone recipe; if they were to tempt tourists, they needed to be right. She practised several times on the family. There were no complaints but a few bulging waistlines.

Extra room was needed for the cafe so Stan set to work on another conversion. This time he sacrificed the family lounge and convinced Kath and Sue it was a small price to pay compared to the potential profit. Stan carefully cleared the room of furniture, distributing it around the rest of the already cluttered house. He then crammed six tables and chairs inside and four outdoors on a makeshift terrace for when the sun shone. Kath sewed pretty gingham tablecloths and bought a collection of plain cups, saucers, side plates and cutlery, adding little home touches like flowers from the garden arranged in glass jars on the table. She then devised and typed the menus.

The small coal-fuelled Aga at the back of the house was kept piping hot and Kath turned out batch after batch of delicious homemade scones and cakes. Stan, sticking to practicalities, got hold of a huge cast-iron kettle and kept it constantly on the boil, ready for teas and coffee. And Sue, between studying for her O-Levels and working at the Wimpy bar, was appointed to the illustrious position of head waitress (she was the only one) and also helped out with the baking.

'I got paid a pound a week and for that I had to muck out two stables, five times a week in on the price!' she said. She quickly worked out she was never going to get rich working for her dad.

As a result of the extra-curricular duties, Sue's education started to suffer. 'Dad said to me, "You can't go to school today, I need someone in the shop." When I told him I had a biology exam, he replied, "What's the point, you're a girl, you're going to get married and have kids. I left school at fourteen and it never did me any harm." That was just the way he was. I guess he was just very old fashioned. He'd lived in Burrough all his life and didn't know any different. It was frustrating for me and even though I admit I wasn't looking forward to doing a biology exam, I should have gone. I never told my mum, I couldn't bear to.'

Stan doggedly pressed on with the tearoom. He made certain passing trade was aware of his new venture by erecting a board outside advertising Sunday Teas and Cakes, encouraging people to stop and enjoy the homemade fare. And he wasn't shy at mentioning the new cafe to whoever came into the shop. 'You can't underestimate the power of word of mouth,' he would say, promoting Kath's cooking to yet another customer.

The first Sunday they opened for business, they were swept off their feet with people queuing up outside for a table. And they kept on coming. Stan and Kath couldn't believe the demand.

'Kath was having to make scones like they were going out of fashion,' said Stan.

Within a few weeks word had spread about the pretty tearoom, the warm welcome and lovely homemade cakes. Parking was easy, it was set in stunning countryside and had an Iron Age fort on the doorstep – a great recipe for a good day out.

Just when Kath thought she was getting a handle on things, the coach parties arrived. People queued around the block and neither Stan nor Kath wanted to turn them away. There was nothing for it – the tearoom had to expand. To the bedrooms!

To avoid the energy-sapping walk up and down the stairs all day, Stan hit on the idea of a dummy waiter to connect the downstairs kitchen to the upstairs bedroom. He drew a basic diagram on the back of his notepad and, after a few nods of approval, set about making and installing it. Kath and Sue tested the contraption, carefully winching hot pots of tea and delicate cakes, checking for spills as they were pulled skywards. When the scones and drinks reached the top they dashed up to inspect the results. 'It was a bit Heath Robinson,' said Sue, 'but it worked.' Now two extra rooms full of happy tourists could be served with the minimum of fuss.

The success of the tearoom and post office had given Stan confidence. He saw huge potential in the catering industry. Having learned so much in a short space of time, he believed there was a market for good honest food, served well and at a reasonable price. The area was bereft of bistro-pubs and restaurant chains, so there was very little in the way of choice for diners. A restaurant with character might really work.

From his window, Stan could see an old pig sty and battered barn, a complete eyesore at the front of Brasenose House. Next to the old buildings lay an abandoned plot of land adjoining the main road. This gave Stan another idea.

In typical fashion, nobody knew what was happening until he walked out of the house with a sledgehammer under his arm.

'He never really talked about his plans, just announced them,' said Sue. Stan joined forces with Jim Reed, a retired builder and stonemason from the village. Having learned his craft at Stimpson builders of Somerby, he was an experienced artisan with time on his hands.

Together they demolished the pig sty and cleared the area, including removing a few dead sheep. Stan was thinking big. He applied for permission to build a restaurant at the front of Brasenose House, using reclaimed bricks from the pig sty.

It was an ambitious plan but permission was granted. Stan and Jim worked day and night to build the hundred-seat restaurant, complete with large picturesque bay window, a flower garden laid by son Philip and ample parking for fifty cars. The heart of the restaurant was one large room, with a sizeable fireplace and parquet dance floor, aimed at attracting big parties.

Stan was granted a liquor licence, installed professional kitchens and then a bar. Burrough Hill Restaurant turned out to be a revelation for the village. Suddenly Stan, sporting his distinctive full goatee beard and now dressed in a dapper waistcoat and colourful bow tie, was a restaurateur.

They came from Melton Mowbray, Oakham, Nottingham and Leicester to dine. The restaurant was one of the few places in the locale that could accommodate large numbers and Stan figured if he could get a few firms' Christmas parties and the occasional wedding reception, he'd soon break even. All the heavy investment and hard work would surely pay off.

Never one for subtlety, Stan stamped his own mark on the interior with classic seventies styling. The large dance room featured garish crimson and gold carpets with vivid patterned curtains and lampshades. Around the bar, psychedelic light panels flashed with alternating red and white bulbs. Smokers gathered on faux leather stools before an array of glass and stainless steel ashtrays and bowls piled high with peanuts. In the main dining area, softly padded chairs covered in brown and white tweed paid homage to the hunting lodge theme. It was an eclectic mix. To show off his equestrian links, Stan added horse brasses, tablemats with steeplechase scenes and framed Dorothy Hardy prints on the walls. On the patio, sunshades billowed hopefully in the breeze.

Stan even commissioned an advertisement announcing the restaurant's five bedrooms, assuring the accommodation was 'elegantly presented'. For good measure he added a little history, 'circa 1703.'

Word spread and the restaurant's reputation grew. Stan's farming connections guaranteed a good supply of quality meat and fresh seasonal vegetables with a Sunday lunch menu that always included Yorkshire pudding, whatever the roast. On some nights, if business appeared a little slow, Stan persuaded Sue to bring her boyfriend along for a meal, so other diners wouldn't be eating alone.

He appointed an experienced chef and kitchen staff with Kath working front of house. They seemed for all the world like the archetypical 'odd couple'. Angela said, 'Stan and Kath were a team but at the same time very different. It was amazing and I've no idea how they made it work!'

Although not a natural raconteur, Stan mastered the art of meeting and greeting. His way was to smile a lot and say as little as possible. 'Those twinkling eyes did most of the work,' said Sue. He'd show people to their tables, sit them down and take their drink order. The choice was diverse including Double Diamond and Mackeson beer, Snowballs, barley wine, and Moet. Stan may have been winging it but he did have a good time – some evenings ending in riotous fun, with alcohol flowing and Stan literally taking over proceedings. 'Stan let us use the restaurant for my mum's retirement,' said Angela. 'He said, "You bring your own food," so everyone from the village brought a dish. Then Stan got his trumpet out. The old headmaster in the village, Mr Underwood, used to have a brass band and started conducting Stan.'

During proceedings Stan opened bottle after bottle of wine and some of the corks were very hard to extract. As an abstemious drinker, Stan had little clue about the quality of wine, but did know which ones needed an extra special effort to open. Once, in Angela's words, 'He pulled so hard he broke wind. The table behind got up and left. Kath came running out, head in hands, saying, "Oh Ange, what will he do next?" '

The large display of alcoholic drinks did not go unnoticed. When the restaurant was burgled, thieves snatched not only the cash box but also helped themselves to Stan's coveted wine cellar.

Although Angela was never officially asked to help out in the restaurant, she knew Stan well enough to see he had split loyalties. 'The restaurant was open most nights but they had to go some to fill it and make it pay, especially as it was competing with the local pub. It was a huge leap for Stan and although it went through a good spell, Stan's horses always came first. He was using money from one thing to subsidise the other.'

It had not been a good year for his horse training career. However hard he tried, a winner looked increasingly unlikely. While Happy Jack had managed a credible third, Green Monkey, though willing, was never going to make first past the post.

Stan had to be honest with himself. With a heavy heart, he relinquished his trainer's licence. He understood there were far better trainers out there and he just couldn't compete. However, he could never abandon horse racing completely. Believing Green Monkey's fine pedigree still had potential, he considered becoming a breeder. After several seasons of love and attention, she had blossomed into a fine specimen, strong and healthy. It was a long shot but definitely worth a punt, so Stan started looking for a good sire to cover Green Monkey. As always, some ideas sound better on paper. There were considerable costs involved and no guarantees. Stan had some serious thinking to do, especially after the investment in the tearoom. He was making a profit but couldn't afford to squander it.

A horse called Richboy, who had won four times out of fourteen starts, had been touted as a possible match for Green Monkey. For around £500 Stan was guaranteed a foal but how it would turn out lay in the lap of the gods. Stan honestly couldn't resist the challenge. He had to find out, even if it came to nothing. He phoned Richboy's owner at Barleythorp Stud and arranged to take Green Monkey over.

Eleven months later, in March 1976, Stan had prepared the stable with a bale of fresh straw and taken to watching Green Monkey like a hawk for any sign of imminent labour. You can't rush nature, although he was most impatient for this birth to happen.

There was nothing unusual about Green Monkey's pregnancy; it was fairly run of the mill. 'There were no problems,' said Sue. 'Dad kept her in the field close to the farm and then moved her into the small yard next to the farmyard.' As her due date got ever closer, Green Monkey started showing signs her foal would soon appear. She was bagging up, her teats and udder enlarged, and she looked uncomfortable as she paced slowly around the yard. 'Dad had set up the empty hay barn – walls on three sides but open onto the yard on the fourth side – with lots of dry straw ready for her to have her foal.' Stan checked on

Green Monkey before going to bed. He lingered that evening until it was dark and then strolled back to the house.

'She was standing in the corner of the barn looking rather resigned to what she knew was going to happen later,' said Stan.

He slept fitfully, a storm overhead disturbing his slumber and awoke to discover the ground soaked. He dressed quickly, eager to check on the mare. Hoping to see Green Monkey waiting eagerly for her bran mash breakfast, he peered into the stables.

She wasn't there. A tingle went down his spine.

He called her name and searched the yard. There she was, standing next to the gate, looking rather pleased with herself. Next to her, lying drenched in a puddle, was a jet black foal struggling to stand.

Stan tenderly lifted the colt back into the stable, laying down extra hay to make it cosy for mare and foal to recover from their ordeal.

'The foal was probably less than an hour old, and although wet, was very alert,' said Sue. 'Dad helped him up onto his feet and then gently guided him into the shelter of the barn. Monkey, always a good mother, followed him in and continued to lick him clean. Dad stayed until the foal had suckled then left them to each other and to recover in peace.'

'He looked nothing special,' Stan said.

7

For the first few days, the new foal remained nameless. Sue had taken to calling him Black Beauty, after the children's novel. Stan still hadn't managed to come up with anything fitting and by the weekend and it was getting to be a family joke. Then, sipping his mug of tea watching the sun set over the fields, it came to him. In the distance the Iron Age fort rose from the peak of the hill, a scene unchanged for generations. This place defined Stan as man and boy; it was a part of his history. 'Burrough Hill Lad,' he whispered. Then once again just to be sure. It sounded right.

He hoped the gangly colt was going to be half as good as the view.

Burrough Hill Lad was handsome, of that there was no doubt; the darkest bay, almost raven black with not a hint of white marking. He certainly had the temperament of his chestnut mare mother, yet he also harboured an unmistakable fire in his young belly.

Sue could tell her father was quietly pleased, even if he wasn't one to gush. She said, 'After a bit Dad concluded the foal was a good size, looked well developed and had attractive colouring.' Soon the process of preparing mother and foal for separation began.

First the young colt was given more freedom. 'After about two or three weeks getting to know each other, Green Monkey and Burrough Hill Lad were moved into the adjacent field during the day and each night brought back into the barn. One month later they were led over tracks to the twenty acre field at the bottom of Burrough Hill, approximately five hundred yards away from the barn,' said Stan.

Green Monkey loved variety and quickly tired of this monotonous routine. She decided to resolve matters by wrenching her head from the rein and making a dash for freedom, but by the time she reached the far end of the field the thrill of escape had long gone. She looked around and realised there was no one for company, her young foal was still on a tight rein over a hundred yards away. Stan held Burrough Hill Lad close to his side and Green Monkey quickly realised if she wanted her foal back, she would have to rejoin them. Crestfallen, she ambled back towards the pair. That moment taught Stan he could not take anything for granted now that Green Monkey was a mother. He had to be even more vigilant. Binoculars always at the ready on his bedroom windowsill, first thing each morning he'd scan the fields, relaxing only after seeing the mare and foal were safe and well.

Still concerned something untoward might happen for the next two months, life revolved around keeping an eagle eye on his favourite horses. 'Every day during May and June, I would drive through the village and down Melton Lane to their field to feed them horse nuts and hay until the grass became plentiful,' said Stan. 'That way I could check all was well and reassure myself.'

Come autumn, the time for Burrough Hill Lad to experience a taste of real independence had arrived. It was a moment Stan dreaded. All his years in farming had taught him such separations are fraught with difficulties. Colts and their mothers do not like being parted, especially when it's the only security they have known.

'After nine months together, they needed to be separated to complete Burrough Hill Lad's weaning,' said Stan. 'So they were both brought into the crew yard and then I led Burrough Hill Lad back up to the farm and into the barn where he was born. Green Monkey was shown into the twenty acre field while Burrough Hill Lad was walked to a different field, Salters Hill, to join another horse for company where he could eat well and grow strong. Although naturally a distressing time for everyone involved, within a few days they settled down well.'

For Sue, this foal was like a storybook come to life. 'I was brought up reading *Black Beauty* and couldn't quite believe I'd now got one in our field!' She spent hours watching Burrough Hill Lad gallop but never had the courage to sit on him. His sheer size and power was evident almost from the moment he was born. 'He was a big gangly thing, but the ground he could cover was amazing. He would tear around the field and during his mad five minutes you'd realise how strong he was. He was such a good looking horse. Dad absolutely loved him.'

The connection between Stan and Buzby, as Burrough Hill Lad had become known, did indeed run deep. In some ways he reminded Stan of himself – not much to write home about at first, but as he grew his natural strength and determination emerged. With Stan's love and attention, the colt developed fast, becoming more muscled and powerful each day, a world away from the bedraggled creature born in a puddle.

He never expected a smooth sailing, but how Burrough Hill Lad would be tamed enough to ride turned out was to tax even Stan's years of experience. All attempts at breaking the horse failed miserably. Burrough Hill Lad could buck all day long. Stan needed help, but for the moment his time and energy were divided as serious problems were emerging at the restaurant.

Burrough Hill Restaurant was turning out to be a huge drain on Stan's resources. Although the business ticked over, cash flow was a constant problem. With inflation spiralling to over seventeen per cent, people didn't have a lot of spare money to spend on domestic bills let alone a night out in a restaurant. Stan had used his dwindling funds to kit out the place and now seriously underestimated the costs it took to keep the doors open: staff, bar stock and the relentless ordering of fresh food.

Being prepared to do everything necessary to stay solvent and see the recession out meant harsh cutbacks. Drastic measures were the only hope of balancing the books. As always, he turned to family to solve the impending crisis.

Kath took over the cooking. Talented chefs cost money and Stan simply couldn't afford them. Putting Kath in charge of the pass was a controversial decision based on economics rather than culinary expertise. According to Angela, 'It wasn't the same. It was so stressful for Kath. She was brilliant doing the teas and making the scones but when it comes to a restaurant meal you had to know what you were doing.'

Stan masked his own lack of knowledge with enthusiasm and a fleetness of foot. 'If people asked Stan to recommend wine or a particular dish he'd dash into the kitchen and ask Kath. She didn't know much more, but she tried. I really think she kept him going for years. She deserved a medal.'

The cutbacks meant staff morale invariably suffered and to reverse the impending air of gloom, Stan tried to raise people's spirits at the Christmas works outing. It was slightly more risqué than usual, the plan being a good laugh would lighten the mood.

'We went to Nottingham,' said Angela. 'Stan said he'd take us to a special club. Well it turns out it was a strip joint. His face! There was a chaise longue on stage underneath a velvet cover but I didn't realise what it was – I asked the waiter what time the raffle was going to be drawn because I thought it was a barrel with numbers in! It was hilarious. A stripper appeared with a black feather boa and as she was pulling it between her legs the feathers were coming off all over the floor. Stan's laughed about that ever since. He's a devil. He reckoned he didn't know – but he damn well did!'

Part two of his economy drive struck closer to home. Paying for holiday accommodation was a luxury they did not need and so Stan converted his estate car into a make-shift hotel. He still took Kath away for a few days, but instead of a cosy bed and breakfast, he put down the seats, pumped up an inflatable mattress and slotted it through the hatchback. Then they'd settle down for the night, unless the traffic woke them. Not exactly the treat Kath hoped for, Stan was just trying his best to keep her happy.

There was one other decision he'd been putting off until last. The horses were too expensive and would have to go. Like a father with a favoured child, Stan knew there was one who would survive the cut: Burrough Hill Lad.

Buzby was his reason to hope, even if he drove him to distraction. First he had to be broken. Stan was an accomplished horseman, riding since he could walk, but this animal really tried his patience. He spent hours trying to make the horse accept the bit, then the saddle, but Burrough Hill Lad always bucked violently. At 16.3 hands, he was not just a strong and muscular beast; there was a stubbornness to match and they were locked in a giant battle of wills. Whatever he tried, however he coaxed; Stan just could not tame him.

As Burrough Hill Lad galloped across the twenty acre field, his massive strides eating up the ground, he looked absolutely unstoppable. There had to be something Stan could do to capture this creature's energy. Tamed, he would be a prize asset. Unbroken, merely a liability.

Reluctantly he made a phone call to a man he knew was a fixer. Geoff Ison from nearby Stonesby had a real knack with horses and a reputation for coaxing even the most troublesome to take the bit. One way of showcasing his success was to place his daughter in the saddle to prove the animal no longer posed a danger. He tried that trick with Burrough Hill Lad and things didn't go quite to plan.

'He bucked her so far up in the air, I thought she'd never come back down again,' Geoff said.

From the start it was clear this wasn't a straightforward job. Geoff often left the field, head collar in hand, shaking his head in disbelief. It didn't go well by anyone's estimation.

Stan began to hint Burrough Hill Lad had turned into an expensive mistake and one day after another unsuccessful session, Geoff offered an alternative solution. He worked for the Honourable Margaret 'Migs' Greenall of Waltham on the Wolds, a brilliant horsewoman who left Scotland during the war to join the Army Remount Depot at Melton and retrain highly-strung thoroughbred horses into jobbing nags. 'We had to convert hunters, and other horses, from riding to harness work, pulling wagons of coke,' she said. 'It wasn't always easy, and I can't say it was good to see hunters tackling such a job – but it had to be done for the war effort.'

Migs Greenall made her home in Leicestershire and became a successful point-to-point rider. She later married Edward Greenall, heir to the Greenall Whitely brewing empire and forged a great bond with her father-in-law, Sir Gilbert, a former Master of the Belvoir Hunt. If anyone understood horses it was Migs. Geoff, knowing Stan was at his wits' end, politely suggested she might be interested in buying Burrough Hill Lad.

'You can have him for £2000,' Stan suggested when they met to tentatively discuss Burrough Hill Lad's future.

She smiled knowingly. 'If you'd asked £12,000 I might have considered it,' she said. 'If he's only worth £2,000, obviously he can't be any good.'

A few days later, Burrough Hill Lad set off across the field and galloped around with more power and speed than ever before. 'My God, that horse has something about him,' Stan thought. It was as if Burrough Hill Lad sensed the danger of being sold and wanted to show what he was capable of.

Stan decided to keep him. On one condition.

After talking with Geoff, they decided to geld the stallion. What Stan would lose in stud fees might be gained on the race track. It was a judgement call. This horse had something special, maybe even the ability to become a good steeplechaser. Yet power and potential meant nothing if he stayed unbreakable.

After the vet had finished his work, Burrough Hill Lad was given time to heal and there were no further attempts to ride him for a while. It was then a gradual process to gain his confidence.

Stan would pat Burrough Hill Lad reassuringly, doing everything as calmly and slowly as he could. He wanted to be the one who would first sit in the saddle. He figured his familiar voice and touch would settle Buzby. So far so good.

Yet almost as soon as Stan climbed onto his back, Burrough Hill Lad kicked his hind legs defiantly in the air, hurling his owner to the ground with a hard and painful thud. Perhaps it was payback time. Stan left the paddock, sore and seriously deflated.

Inside the peace and quiet of the farmhouse, Stan came to the inevitable conclusion there was no way on earth he'd break this obstinate horse without professional help.

He turned to Jimmy Harris, a former jump jockey who rode Green Monkey several years before and was therefore well aware of Burrough Hill Lad's pedigree. Now a trainer, his stable had a growing reputation and was situated just a few miles away at Eastwell, in the beautiful Vale of Belvoir.

Jimmy broke his back in a terrible steeplechase fall at Huntingdon in 1971. Despite lengthy treatment at Lodge Moor Hospital spinal unit in Sheffield, he was unable to walk again. However, he never lost his passion for racing and started a new career as a trainer. His courage impressed many supporters including Lord Oaksey who described Jimmy as 'the gamest pebble of them all'. Even with his disability, Jimmy still helped muck out the stables from his wheelchair. He drew admiration from all fields of life for the way he just got on with the job, never complaining about his lot.

Jimmy's wife, Ann, remembers the day of the accident as if it were yesterday. 'When Jimmy broke his back, our children John and Vicki were only nine and seven. We were all at the race and saw the accident. The owner of Pollock Fair, one of our horses, took me down to Addenbrooke's Hospital following the ambulance, while my sister-in-law took the children home to look after them. After about a week they transferred Jimmy to Lodge Moor spinal unit. We took an everyday round trip from Leicestershire for five months. I tried to be as positive as possible because when you get news like that you have to be, don't you? It's something you learn to live with. The specialists said, "That's it – that's all we can do." It was very different back then. Once he was home, Jimmy refused to go racing. But the owner of Pollock Fair said his horse was running at Southall and wanted Jimmy to come and watch. He said, "He's done no good since you got hurt." So Jimmy went and the horse won. It started his training career because that owner said, "When you get a licence and a yard come and pick him up," which is what we did and that was the first horse we had.'

Jimmy's son, John Harris, said, 'After the accident when I saw him in hospital there was no bitterness. He just lived for horses. When people weren't around and he fell out the chair he'd just climb back in, he was very strong. We worked together. I'd tie the horse up to the ring at the back of the stable and they'd just know he couldn't walk. They wouldn't kick out or anything. A horse like Pollock Fair would chase me out of the stable yet Dad could go in, no trouble. Sometimes he'd say "just follow me". Pollock Fair even had a bit of banter with him and used to get hold of his wheelchair handle!'

Jimmy somehow came to terms with the cards he'd been dealt and tried to turn his misfortune to his advantage. 'In a wheelchair you see more,' he said. 'You pay more attention to what you're looking at. You watch them all; you get to understand them all.'

When Stan asked for help, Jimmy said he was more than happy to train Burrough Hill Lad and Stan immediately felt a weight had lifted. Jimmy had plenty of experience in calming excitable young horses and went back to basics. He put the young horse in the capable hands of Mick Bailey, head lad at the yard, and Mick prepared the way for breaking him in. With Burrough Hill Lad settled on a lead rein, he laid a blanket on his back, gently eased the saddle on and tightened the straps round his belly.

Each step was painstakingly slow. Little by little, trust was gained.

Mick Bailey had a very special relationship with the horses in his care and Burrough Hill Lad turned out to be no exception. They developed a close bond and built trust trotting round the yard side by side, Mick panting hard in an effort to stay abreast. 'He was a big strong horse and all the time he would be jig-jogging,' said Mick. 'He'd never walk. That's why no one wanted to look after him. I had to run everywhere.'

They became faithful friends and Mick had no further trouble after that.

'When he was galloping it was like sitting on a Rolls-Royce. He was something special, I could be cruising and if you pressed a button he'd just go, fly past. But he was so laid back for a nice big horse and rarely got worked up, probably because his mother was a sellingplater.'

Burrough Hill Lad thrived on the attention and enjoyed being ridden by Mick. 'Maybe that was because he loved Polos and I always kept a packet at the ready,' he laughed.

It didn't take long before the gelding was ready to progress to the jumps. Burrough Hill Lad's size and stature weren't always best suited to hurdles, being far from a dainty horse. Natural jumpers are few and far between, however, and what he lacked in innate ability, he made up for with courage and a big heart.

'He was like a machine,' said John Harris. 'It wasn't just speed, it was the pace he could go at and keep on going. As the ground came easier he showed even more class. When most horses hit softer ground it slows them down but with him, it was just the same, he kept going just as fast. He was a real athlete. They don't say there are black horses, they're always called brown, but I don't think you'd get one much darker. Burrough Hill Lad had a lovely temperament, he was as good as gold and didn't have a nasty bone in him.'

Ann Harris explained the secret to keeping Burrough Hill Lad interested was to vary training which stopped him getting bored. 'At Eastwell we could take him up and down Harby Hill, Branston Hill and Stathern Hill. We always gave him plenty of hill work to get him muscled up without doing too much galloping. There were stubble fields all around and we also had Croxton Gallops, so there was something different and new every day. He wouldn't have to do the same thing more than once in a week. All our horses used to love the work. Jim would be out in the car watching them on road exercise and then he'd go onto the gallops with them. Wherever they went, he was always up there with them. When they were on road exercise and out of the village, the lads could jump off and loosen the girth and let them walk up the road, picking at the grass on the way. Then we'd turn them out for a while before they came in to be washed down. After a lunchtime feed they'd be mucked out again, groomed and taken for a walk in the little paddock at the back, then brought in, fed and at about 6 o'clock tucked up for the night.'

Above: Surviving against all odds - Stan as a toddler.

Right: Keen to do his bit, Stan in the Army Cadets.

Left: Stan and Margaret on their wedding day.

Below: The Riley brothers (l-r); Albert, Ken and Stan.

Above: The timber business proved profitable.

Right: Haymaking in summer.

Left: Stan could have been a professional cricket player.

Below: Stan behind the bar at his restaurant.

Left: Stan's horse training was done on a budget.

Above: Stan feeding Burrough Hill Lad as a foal

Left: He looked like Black Beauty and was named after the place he and Stan were born.

Above and left: Burrough Hill Lad and Jenny Pitman, both destined to be champions in their own right.

Right: Johnny Francome clearing a crucial fence on Burrough Hill Lad in the Hennessy Gold Cup.

Below: Phil Tuck savouring the moment.

Above: Cheltenham Gold Cup victory! Phil Tuck and Burrough Hill Lad are guided to the winner's circle.

Right: Phil Tuck, heavily bandaged with a broken nose, before the 1984 Cheltenham Gold Cup.

Below: Stan nervously receiving the Cheltenham Gold Cup from Queen Elizabeth The Queen Mother watched by trainer, Jenny Pitman.

Above: Stan back home with the Cheltenham Gold Cup celebrating with friends.

Left: The new camper van Stan bought with his Cheltenham Gold Cup winnings.

Below: Stan and Jenny holding the Hennessy Gold Cup.

Above: Stan receives the prize for the Charlie Hall Memorial Race, December 1984.

Right: Making headlines as one of the all-time great steeplechasers.

Below: Kath and Stan with Burrough Hill Lad's magnificent trophy collection.

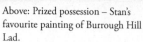

Above: Prized possession – Stan's favourite painting of Burrough Hill Lad.

Left: Taking centre stage during retirement at the hunt with new owner Charlie Warde-Aldam.

Right and below: Stan, now in his eighties, at home in Leicestershire with daughter, Sue.

While Mick schooled him over the gallops at Waltham, Jimmy took care of Burrough Hill Lad's diet, paying great attention to the smallest detail. 'Jimmy used to go out and pick clover and chop it up in the field. Big trainers, they'd chuck the grub in, but Jim would pick dandelions to put in their feed at night.'

The diet tended towards honest food. Jimmy made sure all his horses had homemade bran mash a couple of times a week and for a special treat a horse might have a drop of Guinness or else a few eggs in their feed.

'We always gave them carrots chopped up in the feed along with apples,' said Ann, 'and they all loved lucerne chopped up and mixed in.'

They swore by lucerne for its low sugar levels and high nutrient content, it helped muscle development and speeded up recovery for horses coming back after rest or illness. It made sense that Jimmy always added it to the feed.

The Harris regime worked a treat and finally Stan heard the news he'd waited for: Burrough Hill Lad was ready to be entered into a novice race. Stan didn't need persuading to give the green light. He kept a cool head and hid his true excitement, only asking who the jockey would be. An up and coming rider called Tuck was in the frame.

Philip Charles Tuck was 23 years old and out to prove himself. His learning curve had been steep, but Phil remained determined to make his parents proud.

'When I was a kid I lived in Lincoln and my father was in the building trade,' said Phil. 'He was a racing enthusiast and took me to our local track at Market Rasen. He was very keen on foxhunting and we used to be car followers on a Saturday with many of the local packs. I started riding aged about eight at Major Wall's Riding School in Fiskerton before going to a riding school in Lincoln, run by Arthur Baker called Park Riding School. We'd ride on the Carholme where the Lincoln Handicap used to be run. I pretty well lived there at weekends and school holidays.'

However it was not all plain sailing for young Phil and there were serious doubts he would cope with the demands of horse racing.

'I suffered with asthma and was hospitalized,' said Phil. 'The chest specialist told my parents that I would never be able to work with horses due to all the dust and hay.'

Luckily his parents were not easily dissuaded, feeling it was better he give it a go rather than spend the rest of his life wondering. They crossed their fingers and hoped his breathing problems would disappear as he matured. Their parental intuition proved correct.

'They let me try and I served five years apprenticeship with Walter Wharton near Melton Mowbray. During that time I had five rides, two on the flat and three over hurdles, riding my first winner at Catterick in December 1975.'

Thanks to his parents' brave call, success was now on the horizon with a new trainer.

'I moved to Jimmy Harris and that's where my career started to get going. The first season I had about seventy rides and three winners and over the next three years numbers gradually increased.'

He was the perfect match for Burrough Hill Lad's raw talent, although neither of them knew that a bond was being created. They instantly gelled during their first encounter together at Huntingdon in the Cromwell Novices' Hurdle over two miles. It was hoped the horse's nerves would be calmed on this relatively small, intimate racecourse, especially as the distance was manageable and not too hard a test of the three year-old's fitness.

What no one could predict was how Burrough Hill Lad would react in the midst of all the spectator noise and track hubbub. As he strutted round the parade ring, he appeared to be a little short of conditioning. During the race he made a disappointing start, unable to keep up with the pace. His inexperience was all too obvious and by the finish he'd trailed off some way behind. Despite all expectation it was a highly inauspicious debut.

Undeterred, a week later Burrough Hill Lad was up again, this time at Wetherby where the Romans once raced Arab horses. It was the Thorp Arch Novices' Hurdle, over two miles.

Stan and Jimmy agreed Buzby's learning would accelerate if he was pitted against more experienced competitors. On this occasion Phil had to give up the saddle to Gordon Holmes. Unfortunately, the change of jockey made no difference and it was almost a repeat performance – Burrough Hill Lad had a poor start and never really got going. In fact, Stan was concerned at how little energy the horse appeared to have as he again tailed off towards the end of the race.

Back home, discussions between Stan and Jimmy centred on realizing Burrough Hill Lad's untapped potential. Neither doubted he had the ability. It was a matter of working on his endurance.

Fourteen days later, on 15 November, after overnight rain, the going was soft at Stratford where Burrough Hill Lad was running in the Southern Cross Novices' Hurdle, again over two miles. Phil was back in the saddle and maybe Burrough Hill Lad was more comfortable with the familiar, because despite running a one-paced race in foggy conditions, he just kept on going, strong and focused right through the finish line. He came a creditable third.

It was the breakthrough they'd been hoping for. After a trio of races, his stamina appeared to be improving. Could the tide be turning?

Back in Burrough, the Christmas period at the restaurant was frenetic with parties, diners and dancing. Kath and Stan put in long hours but nothing was going to deter them from rising at the crack of dawn on Boxing Day to drive to Market Rasen. They arrived bleary eyed yet hopeful of good things.

Burrough Hill Lad was running in the Accurate Junior Novices' Hurdle over two miles with Jonathan Haynes as the jockey. After the last race, things looked encouraging. Jimmy had worked him hard over the past couple of weeks and Burrough Hill Lad's form had markedly improved during training. Would it translate to the racetrack? Many believed so and they weren't the only ones impressed by Burrough Hill Lad's condition as a fair bit of money was laid on him. Stan thought the odds sounded pretty good so throwing caution to the wind he dug deep to have, what for him, was a considerable bet. 'I had £50 on him to win at 50/1.'

Burrough Hill Lad started quite brilliantly, making great headway. With two hurdles to go, he was in the lead. Stan and Kath cheered nervously from the stands, willing him on with every stride. Stan felt for his betting slip and Kath crossed her fingers. But at the last, horse and rider completely misjudged the jump and the jockey tumbled head over heels, sprawling onto the turf.

They were stunned as Stan looked on in weary disappointment. He'd just kissed goodbye to a much-needed £2,500.

In the enclosure, Stan and Jimmy focused on the positives. Burrough Hill Lad had made amazing progress and he showed clear potential to win. They both knew it. Now all they had to do was get the jumps right; get those gangly legs of his clear over every damn fence.

There wasn't much time. Burrough Hill Lad had only a week to recover.

1980 dawned, a new decade and a new era. On 5 January Stan travelled back to Market Rasen for the Grimsby Novices' Hurdle over two miles. It may have been the same racecourse but there was a new-found confidence about Burrough Hill Lad.

The horse paraded around as if knowing he was special. From the off it was clear Burrough Hill Lad was in excellent form. Phil Tuck rode a stormer, holding him back until three hurdles out. When the other riders tried to up the momentum, he let him have his head. Burrough Hill Lad shot off like a rocket and romped home, twenty lengths in the lead, winning over £500 in prize money.

Stan had done it! After thirty years, he had finally produced a winner. 'I had to read it in the papers the next day before it sank it,' he said.

Despite the doubters, Stan's self confidence never deserted him. 'I thought a winner would come along sooner or later, I just hoped it would be sooner!'

Just three days later they were at Leicester Races. After the excitement of Market Rasen, Stan decided to make a day of it and offered to take Angela along as company for Kath. They all piled into his car, leaving Angela's mum to look after the post office. 'I was supposed to be working that day,' said Angela, 'so it was a surprise when Stan asked me to go with him. When we got to Leicester, Kath said she didn't want to get out of the car and stayed inside knitting! Maybe she was nervous. I rang my husband and said, "Look, Stan's taken me to the races because Burrough Hill Lad is running." He urged me to put the housekeeping on it, saying, "He must be onto a win if he's taking you!" '

Angela fiddled nervously with the money in her purse, wondering what to do for the best. A small windfall would be very welcome but she couldn't decide whether to take her husband's advice. Waiting until the very last minute, she walked forward with several notes in her hand, but overcome with thoughts of all her bills back home, instead used the small change in her pocket as a stake.

This time Peter Scudamore had been asked to ride Burrough Hill Lad in the Croxton Park Novices' Hurdle over two miles. He rode a textbook race, leading from the second last. When he hit the front, Angela could hardly bear to watch, a sick feeling in her stomach. How could she face her husband? After Burrough Hill Lad romped home by fifteen lengths, she collected the meagre winnings. She couldn't stop thinking what might have been!

Stan was elated. Like the proverbial bus, he waited years for a winner and now two had come along in three days. What were the chances of getting three out of three?

On 18 January at Kempton Park, Stan was both exited and anxious. Burrough Hill Lad had an air of self-assurance but was pitted against another up and coming horse called Corbiere, trained by Jenny Pitman, an old acquaintance of Stan. Achieving great success as one of the few female trainers, Jenny had a great gift: an uncanny understanding of horses.

This race was a step up for Burrough Hill Lad and the first time he'd run over three miles. The acid test. Once more there was a change of jockey – Steve Knight took the saddle.

Buoyed by recent success, Stan once again decided to have a bet. He just couldn't resist. Burrough Hill Lad started well, up there with the leaders. Pacing steadily to ensure he went the distance, towards the last he was neck and neck with Corbiere. Stan knew Burrough Hill Lad had a turn of speed over the final furlong and waved his ticket furiously in anticipation of a wonderful victory.

The two horses leapt together, side by side, the thunderous sound of hooves echoing around the track. With one hurdle left, a single jump to triumph, Stan held his breath. Corbiere cleared it well, emerging unscathed, but Burrough Hill Lad wasn't so fortunate – his giant body somersaulted and smacked into the turf head first, his powerful neck receiving an almighty blow.

The crowd expected the big black horse to jump up, but Burrough Hill Lad didn't move and lay on the ground twitching. Stan feared the worst. Each second seemed an eternity.

Stable lad Mick Bailey rushed onto the track, one of the first to reach Burrough Hill Lad. 'By the time I got there he was still on the floor,' said Mick. 'I thought he was going to be shot. I thought he was a gonner.'

Jenny Pitman said, 'It was an X-certificate fall, with the horse landing vertically on his head. He'd not moved for five minutes – in fact there was a big cheer from the crowd when he got up on his feet.'

A short while later, Jenny came over and asked Jimmy how Burrough Hill Lad was faring. 'Not at all good, Jenny,' he replied. 'He can't pick his neck up more than two feet off the ground.' She suggested contacting Ronnie Longford, an equine chiropractor and renowned expert.

Stan pushed his way towards Burrough Hill Lad, who was now in so much pain he could barely raise his head.

The awkward landing had badly distorted his body and concerned looks from bystanders expressed the unthinkable – was this a survivable injury?

John Harris said, 'When he fell it was like his head was displaced from his neck. He dislocated his vertebra. He couldn't walk, they could hardly get him on the loading ramp to the horsebox and take him home he was in such a bad way. He was in so much distress there was talk of putting him down.'

Having painstakingly coaxed Burrough Hill Lad into the box, the journey home was long and arduous. They drove slowly, smoothly changing gears to cause as little discomfort as possible to the horse. No one knew how this was going to play out. Hope was fading fast.

'It took ages to get him back to the stables and then he just stood there with his head down,' Mick Bailey said.

The call went out for help, and before long they were doing exactly what Jenny suggested, slowly weaving their way to Ronnie Longford's surgery.

'The minute Ronnie Longford saw him, he didn't even take him out of the horse box,' John said. 'My dad was already in there. Ronnie joined him and said the horse's head was on wrong, like it was nearly dislodged from the top of his ears to his spine.'

Ronnie certainly knew his stuff. As a young boy he turned up for school every day on the back of a pony. He had served in the desert with the Warwickshire Yeomanry where he developed a skill for nursing crippled horses back to full health. So when he strode onto that lorry, he wasn't at all fazed by Burrough Hill Lad's predicament and set straight to work. A crash, a bang, then a series of strange noises emanated from the box. The team, waiting anxiously outside, worried all the more.

Ronnie carried on, undeterred. He'd learnt his trade alongside a famous chiropractor and became so adept at curing spinal problems that his services were soon in high demand. 'I used to go to Ireland once a fortnight, then to see the bullfighters' horses in Spain and the showjumpers' horses in Greece as well as race horses in Barbados and Trinidad. I've been all around the world. I'm not a vet, I'm just an old farmer's boy.'

One look at Burrough Hill Lad and Ronnie knew exactly what was wrong. He reckoned by manipulating the bones back into place there would be instant relief. Running his hands over the horse's neck he discovered the exact place of the dislocation.

'He was wrong in the front of his withers,' said Ronnie, 'and would definitely have had to be put down because he couldn't raise his head. So I put the bones back with my hands. I gave it one click with the heel of my hand.'

His examination also revealed another problem – one of Burrough Hill Lad's legs was out of place. Ronnie then said to Jim, 'He's alright. But has he always turned that leg out?' Jim replied, 'Do you know, I've never really noticed.' Ronnie studied the joint for a moment, then flicked it and readied himself to manipulate the bones.

'I did the near shoulder by lifting the leg up and rotating it,' said Ronnie.' It doesn't take a lot of strength;

it's just about getting the angle right. You have to pull it forward and rotate it in a little tiny circle not more than a foot or eighteen inches.'

The result was not just a relief for Burrough Hill Lad, but everyone around. 'The horse jumped in that much shock, I think his neck jolted back on. As he came off the lorry he was virtually nearly normal straight away,' said John, 'and then Ronnie said to the lad, "Trot him up." Away he went and never had any more bother.'

Ann Harris could hardly believe it was the same horse she had seen in agony just a few moments before. 'Ronnie said he'd do a few bits and bobs while the horse was in the lorry. And you've never heard so many cracks and bangs. Then blow me, if the horse didn't walk out!'

The next time Jenny bumped into Jimmy, he happily reported Burrough Hill Lad's recovery was nothing short of miraculous. Stan began to wonder if Burrough Hill Lad had nine lives.

What the horse needed now was decent rest and the chance to recuperate slowly. During his recovery, John noticed Burrough Hill Lad was moving in a very strange way. 'He was a good ride but he had this little thing, he used to lock up his hind leg up and couldn't put it to the floor. He'd be hopping along on three legs and you'd think, "What has he done?" Every now and again it happened. Then it would let go and he'd be away. He'd only do it walking or trotting, but cantering or galloping he'd be fine. It was something he couldn't control, like a leg seizure.'

The fall at Kempton delivered another salutary lesson for Stan – fixing an injured horse costs a lot of money. And there were no promises Burrough Hill Lad would ever be right again, let alone able to race. The stark reality was some horses never jump after a fall like that. They either don't recover fully or simply lose their nerve.

They wouldn't know for a while whether Burrough Hill Lad had a future or was set for early retirement. With the off season fast approaching, Stan transported his horse back on to home turf. Was it best to cut his losses? He could hardly fund a horse in tip-top health, let alone one felled by serious injury.

Jimmy encouraged Stan to believe things would turn out alright. John said, 'My dad sent him back with a couple of month's supply of food and stuff because he was a big horse. Dad said, "Don't just leave him on grass." We always knew Stan couldn't afford the horse and training, so we helped him along. Even before he raced, Stan said, "I don't think I can afford it any longer, I think I'll have to sell him." My dad said, "I think you've got a good one here, best hang onto him." '

Jimmy suggested the best way forward was for Stan to feed Burrough Hill Lad a mixture of highly nutritious oats and nuts to strengthen him up for the next season. So every other week the stable prepared and delivered the mix which gave them an excuse to pop by and ensure their prodigy was in rude health. Ann said they created a production line especially for Burrough Hill Lad, but he was such a fine horse, he was worth it.

At the beginning of summer, Jimmy wanted Burrough Hill Lad returned, in preparation for next season's training. 'We'll come and fetch him to make a start,' he said during a phone call to Stan.

'No, it's alright, I've already sent him to Harry Wharton in Wetherby.'

Jimmy was knocked for six. 'Dad wished he had rung up sooner,' said his son, John.

Stan revealed that there was nothing purposefully secretive about the move; it was purely a matter of convenience. 'There was never any problem with Jimmy Harris, it was simply Harry Wharton came highly recommended by my old friend and best man, Harry Matthews.'

A long-time friendship had triumphed over a professional partnership. However, it was a union that was short-lived. Winning twice in eleven days, first at Uttoxeter, then Cheltenham, did not satisfy Stan.

Now he understood. He realized he didn't want to win, he wanted to win big. Time to get going.

8

The 1970s ended with the election of the first female British Prime Minister, Margaret Thatcher. Women were in power and men had to get used to it. Local girl Jenny Harvey was blazing her own trail. Her father, George, was a dairy farmer in Hoby, and from an early age, Jenny was happiest watching mighty shire horses plough the fields. The fourth of seven children, Jenny was a tomboy and horse mad. Her father allowed her to ride their trusted carthorse, Nellie, when she was only two.

Stan had known her for many years, ever since she took part in pony races at her neighbour's farm which by coincidence belonged to Stan's oldest brother, Albert.

Stan would drive over to see his big brother without mentioning he'd actually come to admire the horses. Albert didn't mind, there was a light-hearted side to him and, being one of three brothers, he often played the role of prankster. He also set up kiddies' pony races and got local children to take part as jockeys. Jenny Harvey was one such rider.

'Albert devised a handicap system and organised a bookmaking system on the outcome of the races,' Jenny said. 'We took our ponies' abilities very solemnly.'

However, despite his best efforts Albert's days as a race fixer were numbered. 'This caper would have continued for many months,' said Jenny, 'but my cousin incurred a nasty fall. It did not best please my parents and they put a swift end to our exploits.'

Their wrath was short-lived. Not long after Jenny stabled her point-to-pointer, Dan Archer, at Albert's farm in exchange for helping out around the yard. There was only ever going to be one career path for Jenny – one that involved horses. One of her first jobs was as stable girl at Bishop Cleeve in Cheltenham where she met and later married Richard Pitman, a jockey. Talented and tenacious, by the time she was thirty Jenny Pitman had set up her own stables at Upper Lambourn in the virtually derelict Weathercock House and quickly built a reputation as one of the best trainers the racing world had ever seen.

Stan knew Jenny understood horses like no one else and that she would fight for them like they were her own children. Old-fashioned when it came to a woman's place,

Stan was nevertheless a realist – Jenny trained her horses to win.

'It takes guts, determination and courage to attempt to do a man's job in a man's racing world,' said Jenny. Exactly the type of fighting talk Stan loved. 'I can look at a horse the way most women look at a house they're going to buy,' she added. 'They see the frame and know just how it's going to look when they've built on it.'

Stan was hooked. There was no one like Jenny, a rising star who had already notched up eighty victories by the time he called. Stan prayed she'd take on his protégée. Burrough Hill Lad was still jumping in that awkward way of his over fences – all legs. Jenny more than anyone would know what to do. Sue saw it as the perfect match. 'In a way, Jenny was the best person to understand Dad. She could see problems coming before he did.'

Jenny agreed to take a look at Burrough Hill Lad and quickly identified her concerns. 'He stood terribly straight in front. His foreleg came straight down from his shoulder joint and straight up from his fetlock joint – if you'd dropped a plumb line it could not have been straighter. Conformation like that puts more strain on the legs.'

Jenny also noticed scarring on Burrough Hill Lad's hind leg, the result of running into barbed wire during one of his mad five minutes as a youngster. Although the wound was old, even when she touched it ever so lightly, Burrough Hill Lad flinched. Clearly it was still incredibly sensitive and he moved oddly to protect it. Jenny watched closely and saw Burrough Hill Lad shielding this old injury by swinging his off-hind outwards to stop it coming into contact with his other leg. As a result he placed extra weight onto the front legs, making his whole gait awkward and unbalanced. Jenny was surprised he was managing to run at all, never mind at speed!

She would have to correct this problem, but also saw there was plenty to work with. 'When you looked at his action from the side, rather than behind, he was the most unbelievable athlete. He trotted with a very straight action and covered an enormous amount of ground with each stride,' said Jenny.

Stan was sold on Jenny and just had to find the money to hire her. It was the off-season and Stan spent the next few weeks juggling the books to see how he could afford expert training for Burrough Hill Lad. He looked ever more closely at how to make savings in the restaurant.

Stan tried many times to persuade Angela to come and work at the restaurant but she dug her heels in, determined to retain her position in the post office. She feared that, despite Stan's best efforts, things were heading one way – downhill. Even the simplest things seemed to be going wrong. 'My mum used to clean the kitchen and it didn't help when she poured what she assumed was a jug of dirty water down the sink, only to find out it was the latest batch of freshly-made stock. That didn't go down too well!'

Stan tried not to over-think his financial woes. With his back against the wall and on the brink of fulfilling an ambition, he refused to give up on Burrough Hill Lad.

Having been denied opportunity by a strict father, he saw this as his last chance to make a mark in racing. It was apparent the horse had a hold on his heart as well as his wallet.

'He was such a lovely horse and Stan was as proud as punch of him,' said Angela. 'I was taking my dog on a walk from Burrough to Great Dalby and Stan appeared with Burrough Hill Lad. My God – he was striding out and there was no way I could keep up, so I just let them go. I never knew Stan could move that quick!'

While Stan was in control of the training programme, he tried everything to keep Burrough Hill Lad in tip-top condition. He rode Burrough Hill Lad every day without fail, often having to use all his wit and strength to keep the powerful horse under control.

'I was not easily scared when I rode Burrough Hill Lad, even when he bucked,' Stan said. 'He was really the most fantastic ride.'

However, Burrough Hill Lad didn't understand how strong he really was. 'Once I needed to get him in from the field when it was snowing like hell, a complete blizzard,' said Stan. 'I wanted to get him back to the yard. So I got some oats to persuade him and when I finally took the bowl away he lashed out with his back leg. Later on I had to serve in the restaurant with one arm in plaster and tell everyone I'd slipped off a ladder in the stock room.'

Stan had wanted sporting success for as long as he could remember. It was now or never. Having finally made up his mind, there was no small talk or preamble, he simply picked up the phone to Jenny. 'He's ready to start cantering now. Would you like to train him for me?'

Jenny didn't hesitate either. She relished a challenge and this was a big one.

Now Burrough Hill Lad was part of her stable, Jenny wasted no time. She tried a series of boots to protect the horse's injured leg but that merely produced the opposite effect to the one she wanted. The boots irritated the delicate scar tissue and Burrough Hill Lad just threw his leg out even further. Back to the drawing board.

Whilst jumping, Burrough Hill Lad could get any amount of height but his timing and stride pattern were utterly hit and miss. Jenny noticed when he approached a fence right, he would sail over. If he came up too close, he would carry on as if it wasn't there. He'd smack straight into the fence 'like a tank had gone through it', sending the jockey flying.

'He'd never bother to change his stride,' said Jenny. 'If he met it right he was brilliant. If not, he didn't give a stuff.'

Jenny decided to send him back to school in an attempt to re-learn everything. First, she led him over poles laid on the ground, then gradually progressed to tiny fences only two feet high, aimed at not only sorting out his approach but helping him sense what it felt like to jump properly. It was a painstakingly slow process.

Jenny needed immense staying power and the patience of a saint to deal with Burrough Hill Lad. Every day seemed like two steps back and one forward. It was obvious he was never going to be technically brilliant but, gradually, more often than not he jumped right over the fences with room to spare. And his easy temperament made everyone warm to him as the archetypal gentle giant. Out on the gallops, Burrough Hill Lad's powerful engine was evident. He could easily outpace every other horse in Jenny's stable. If Jenny could bottle that energy and keep his legs in check, this horse could make it into the record books. Groom Andrew Scobie Jones was brought in to keep a special eye on Jenny's latest addition.

'The flat was boring and I wanted to get back to jump racing,' he said. 'One of the head lads was a good friend of Jenny Pitman's. He told her I was looking for a job and she rang me. "Scobe," she says. "Yeah." "It's Mrs P." "Oh, hello Mrs P." "I've got a horse I want you to look after. I can't tell you he'll win the Gold Cup, but he'll definitely run in it." "I'm in!" '

With that Scobie Jones took over Burrough Hill Lad's main duties, which included preparing and riding him during training runs. Buzby's nonchalant attitude belied his strength of character and it was down to Scobie to unleash the wolf in sheep's clothing.

'He didn't look a lot in the box, dipped back, high withers, big bone head on him. Then you'd sit on and ride him and think he doesn't feel like a lot either. You'd walk down to the gallops and he'd start pumping on two cylinders, he'd go up to four, then he'd drop his head and his neck would pop out and his shoulders would pop in front of you and you'd think, Jesus Christ, I'm on a different bloody horse! He hated getting beat. Whether he was on the gallops or trotting up the road in the morning, if he saw something in front of him, he had to get in front of them. We'd pull out at half past seven at the same time as Fred Winter's horses and they'd be half a mile down the road from us. When he saw them he was a nightmare to ride. I had to turn round and come back, otherwise he wouldn't settle on the way home. He just had to get in front of everything.'

In order to keep costs down, Stan bought an old campervan so he could travel to the races and stay overnight in the vehicle. He invited Sue to tag along and she was happy to come and enjoy the fun.

'It had a pop-up roof, which meant I could sleep in a sleeping bag on the ledge bed above Dad and Kath, who had the double bed below, once the table had been folded away. It was very cramped but we did sleep reasonably well. There was no toilet, no shower, just a small sink, a couple of gas rings and a cool box. Definitely no TV. In the mornings we'd boil a small kettle to make a brew and make breakfast – bacon, sausage, mushrooms and egg with slices of bread and butter or else bacon butties in a small frying pan. We all got on very well. Kath could also rustle up sandwiches if necessary, although takeaway pie and chips or fish and chips were relied upon in the evenings. And Dad would park up almost anywhere for the night; car parks, lay-bys even, but if possible fairly close to a public toilet.'

Burrough Hill Lad's first race for Jenny Pitman was on 18 November 1981 at Kempton, the same racecourse where he had fallen onto his neck almost two years before as Corbiere hurtled over the finish line to victory.

Stan banished all thoughts of that disastrous race. 'I'd moved on and was feeling excited and positive,' said Stan. 'The important thing was to see if Burrough Hill Lad was going to perform as Jenny predicted.'

It was a handicap hurdle over three miles. Even with Phil Tuck on board, it was a fairly inauspicious start, and didn't get much better. The race was won by Grand Hussar and Burrough Hill Lad trailed in fifth, running out of gas at two out.

Jenny continued to work on his fitness and, more importantly, tried to dampen Stan's high expectations.

'If she didn't agree with him, she would argue,' said Sue. 'Dad likes strong women and Jenny is a strong woman. She'd play along with his little games until she'd had enough then say, "Now come on Stan!" '

Each subsequent race saw Burrough Hill Lad improve. First Newbury, then Nottingham. Then Leicester, where he came second. Things were better, but nowhere near what Stan or Jenny wanted.

Three months passed and a new year arrived. On 16 February 1982 at Newton Abbot, Burrough Hill Lad was entered for the Rippon Tor Novices' Chase. With two to go, jockey Colin Brown eased Buzby past the favourite, Drop's O'brandy and romped home to an easy win. Victory!

It felt really good, but Stan dared not get his hopes up again quite yet. The next race was in Liverpool on 1 April. All Fool's Day. He drove up in the small camper along with Kath and Sue deciding to make a long weekend of it and hunted around for cheap places to park at night.

'We were away for three nights,' said Sue. 'It was a heck of a squash but great fun. First night we stayed on a residential street in Liverpool; the second on a beach front at Southport where we were woken up by something going on outside. I looked out the window and there was Ginger McCann's string of racehorses going past for their morning workout. The third night we parked at the Aintree racecourse. We pushed up the pop up roof and settled in. In the morning there was a loud hailer announcement: "Would the campervan please lower its lid because we can't see enough of the fence." '

After having quickly moved the van, Stan and Sue took off towards the track.

'Dad and I walked the course. It was the night before the Grand National and these naughty young lads were pulling chunks out of the fence. We reported it to a nearby policeman who didn't seem that interested. The next morning it was all over the newspapers that some fences had been damaged and one set on fire!'

Burrough Hill Lad was running in the Siematic Kitchen Novices' Chase and Stan soon felt deflated when all Buzby's bad habits looked like they were coming back to haunt him. Leading with ease for the majority of the race, he mistimed the thirteenth and slipped back. Just as Stan was giving up hope, Burrough Hill Lad produced a turn of speed over the last and hauled back the leaders overtaking them all to win in grand style.

Scobie Jones said, 'He took the third last clean out the ground, broke the back rail and put a four foot hole in it and still got up and won. He just went through it like a bloody bulldozer.'

It was a game changer. It was also an eye-opener for the Riley family. A rush of victory coursing through their veins, they couldn't stop smiling for the rest of the afternoon. They decided to quietly make their way home. Just as they were leaving, Jenny Pitman called them over and suggested they join her for a drink.

'Another owner was there dripping in gold and drinking champagne,' said Sue, 'and although they were lovely people it really made me think. They hadn't even won, yet were happy to celebrate with us.'

They were in new territory at the Foxwell Novices' Chase at Newton Abbot on 12 April. Stan was sitting in his campervan when he heard Burrough Hill Lad was the favourite and almost choked on his cornflakes. Back in the saddle, Phil Tuck did not disappoint and strode clear by twelve lengths. Things were looking good.

Yet amidst all the excitement settled a strange calm that often accompanies success, the feeling this was simply how it was meant to be. Jenny ticked all the boxes and Stan finally accrued some winnings to pay for the horse of his dreams. Maybe the stars were at last aligned in their favour.

No one could have predicted what happened next. It came completely out of the blue and shocked the world. Horse racing was thrown into absolute disarray when Shergar, the highest valued horse in Europe, became headline news for the wrong reason.

The Aga Khan owned and bred Shergar in Ireland and the colt went on to win the 1981 Derby, thrashing the opposition by over ten lengths – an unheard of margin for such a prestigious race. He won the Irish Derby ridden by Lester Piggott with such ease commentator Peter O'Sullevan exclaimed, 'He's only in an exercise canter!'

The accolades kept coming. After Shergar's eight-race career, the Aga Khan sold 34 shares in the horse for £250,000 each and kept six for himself. That valued Shergar at a mind blowing £10 million.

On 8 February 1983, three balaclava-clad men forced their way into the County Kildare stud where Shergar was kept. At gunpoint they threatened James Fitzgerald, Shergar's groom, and demanded he lead them to the horse. His wife and family were held hostage in the house. 'Call the police and you die!' they warned. Shergar was eventually coaxed by a terrified Fitzgerald into a horse box and driven away through the foggy night, never to be seen again.

It was later surmised from the £2 million ransom demand, the guns, passwords and size of the gang to be the work of the IRA. However, it is doubtful any of the kidnappers knew how to handle such a highly strung horse and Shergar's sad fate was sealed. Extensive searches yielded no trace of the animal. A report by the Aga Khan concluded Shergar was dead within a week. Despite never finding his remains, it is believed he was shot. Shergar's fate sent panic throughout the racing world and suddenly security became an obsession.

Video surveillance, extra guards and sophisticated locks were introduced in top racing stables. Jenny Pitman took every possible precaution to safeguard the horses in her care, including Burrough Hill Lad.

There was turmoil in the Riley household too. A few months after Shergar's disappearance, Stan called it a day at the restaurant. To avoid bankruptcy, the business had to go. Midweek trade had fallen away, Kath's health was suffering and they were simply not able to create enough income to sustain the business. The stark reality of a gloomy profit and loss sheet could not be denied. On the brink of losing everything, including Burrough Hill Lad, Stan closed it down.

After a lifetime in Burrough, Stan wanted to start afresh somewhere new. First they had to sell – everything. From Stan's prize trumpet to the horse brasses, it all went up for auction. Meticulous to the last, Kath noted the price of every item sold in red biro next to its listing in the hastily prepared catalogue.

By 10.30 in the morning on 2 September 1983, the restaurant car park was full and a large crowd gathered. No one had come to eat. They were all keenly awaiting the raising of the auctioneer's gavel. It was going to be a busy day for Walker Walton Hanson.

Every single item connected with the restaurant was up for sale. To help proceedings speed along, a 26-page pamphlet costing 50p had been printed listing all the items starting with lot one, 'a large quantity of deep crimson and gold dutch floor tiles (good quality and condition)' which eventually sold for £28.

The coat racks and horse brasses, candlesticks and four-seater settee sold quickly, as did the rolls of electric cable, emergency lights and fire extinguisher. By the time they got to the 'sparklet cream whipper' (which fetched £6) the auctioneer was well into his stride. He'd now described over 160 lots and raised more than £3000, yet there were almost 350 lots to go and no break for lunch.

The cash register fetched £75, while a 'metal castrator' struggled to reach over a fiver. However, the Formica-fronted bar with a wood simulated top proved popular with several bids raising the price to £85. Then it was back to basics again with a towel rail going for a pound. Out went all the alcohol – Guinness, Snowballs, Blue Nun, champagne and whisky.

Downsizing for Stan and Kath meant goodbye to the lawn mower (£180) and a huge array of tools. Although sad to see all these items go, it generated a good source of cash and cleared out their clutter. By the time they got to Lot 508, the Galvanised Tank (£2), everyone was exhausted.

All that was left was to find somewhere to live.

9

Buying a bungalow made day-to-day living a little easier. For Kath, there were no stairs to climb, no temperamental central heating boiler to coax into life and no more worries about cooking to restaurant standards. And for Stan, it promised a simpler lifestyle with open views across the Cropston fields. The last few months had been very stressful. However, they had settled their debts, letting no one down. It was the honourable thing to do. For the time being they could live off the surplus from the sale of the restaurant and Brasenose House. With no other income, Stan staked his future on Burrough Hill Lad.

To keep outgoings to a minimum, during the off-season Stan brought Burrough Hill Lad back to the rented pasture land. While a controversial decision to remove a horse from training stables, for Stan it was the pragmatic thing to do. Anyway, he didn't have another choice.

Sue enjoyed having Buzby back. 'When Burrough Hill Lad came home for the summer it was like his annual holiday. He was turned out in a twenty acre field with a couple of others for company. It was the field where he'd spent his first few months with his mum, so he was familiar with it. He lazed about, ate lots of grass and put on weight. It made sense as it was cheaper than paying for someone else to put him out to grass.'

Towards the end of August, training resumed. At first it consisted of gentle exercise, enough to work off the excesses of summer before increasing the intensity to more strenuous building muscle and endurance.

'About three to four weeks before he returned to Jenny, I'd bring him in and begin our roadwork,' said Stan. 'We'd start at eight every morning, saddle up and go for a long walk, just on our own. We'd usually do a four or five mile round trip up to Cold Overton via Somerby and back, or to Great Dalby, Thorpe Satchville and then Twyford.'

To Stan it was much more than training. He now had time to really indulge his favourite horse all the while knowing he was set to face the biggest challenge of his racing career.

Sue watched the two of them return, looking like they didn't have a worry in the world. 'They'd even settle down and have breakfast together when they got back,' she said.

But for Stan his was a cleverly calculated gamble. By removing the stress and lessening demands on the animal, he reasoned there was a better chance his horse would enter the next season in the very best of health. It may not have been conventional, but he combined his experience as a permit trainer and the tips Albert had passed on down the years to create his own unique equine programme. 'I never learned what to do from reading a book!' said Stan.

Back in Lambourn, Jenny didn't like the arrangement. She thought Stan's regime was unlikely to bring out the best in the horse and complained repeatedly that Stan's economy drive was detrimental to their joint aim. She made no bones about reminding Stan he should leave training to the professionals.

'I was told it wasn't fair on the horse and it wasn't fair on me,' Stan said. And despite Stan's idiosyncratic techniques there were indeed times when Burrough Hill Lad refused to play ball, even, after all their years together. 'Once he fly bucked me on the old railway line at John O'Gaunt, all the way down the steep railway bank. I had to lie still on his back just to stay on.' It was a warning Stan failed to heed. He never worried about riding Burrough Hill Lad, it felt like second nature.

Yet one day, soon after the railway incident, even Stan began to have serious doubts. Trotting through the village, making their way down the Twyford Road, everything seemed fine. The horse was perfectly calm and moving nicely. Until, suddenly, he violently reared up for no apparent reason.

'I was really frightened,' said Stan. 'I struggled to keep control and then he bucked me half way up his neck. I remember thinking all he had to do was drop his neck, I'd go over and land head first and be in a wheelchair for life.'

Fortunately, Burrough Hill Lad stayed upright and Stan carried on, albeit considerably shaken. He decided the horse had just been spooked as he recalled Jenny's wise words. 'She always said he wasn't nasty, just liked to show how strong he was.'

Safely back home, Stan went over and over what had happened and came to the conclusion enough was enough. Having seen his fair share of devastating injuries, the incident persuaded Stan he could no longer carry on. It was time to let the professionals take over. Jenny finally got her way and Burrough Hill Lad went back to Lambourn sooner than planned.

Stan justified the decision by saying if his horse was half as good as everyone believed then he was set to win decent prize money, which would fund the extra fees. It was time to cut his losses. And save his own skin.

For Jenny, having Burrough Hill Lad back in her yard of 29 horses was a real bonus. A horse with such ability who could also make people laugh was great for morale. After a good work out, Burrough Hill Lad would entertain the troops with his own comedy routine. 'He would plunge his head into his water bucket right up to his eyes,' said Jenny. 'He looked like a hippopotamus, then he'd blow down his nostrils so the water exploded.'

With the 1983-4 season fast approaching, it was back to business and Jenny was keen to enter Burrough Hill Lad in more prestigious races. He'd made good, steady progress over the past season and needed to be stretched if he was going to show his mettle.

The Welsh National in Chepstow immediately after Christmas was chosen as the one to aim for and Stan couldn't wait. Jenny's stats now showed she had trained over one hundred winners. Just a few months before, star of the stable Corbiere had done her proud by winning the Grand National at Aintree. Her stock had never been higher. She was fast becoming a legend.

Corbiere and Burrough Hill Lad were ideal stable-mates. Jenny trained them together and after a gallop at Wolverhampton was impressed enough to predict, 'Burrough Hill Lad will win the Coral Welsh National. He is well handicapped and I can't see the top ones giving him the weight.'

She had utter conviction. And while it was usual for trainers to be quietly confident, it was refreshingly honest of Jenny to tell anyone who would listen when she thought her stable would triumph. The bookies and punters loved it. Not one to mince words, she spread the news there was something exceptional about Burrough Hill Lad, now easily out pacing Corbiere, a horse that could stay and stay.

Over the years, several jockeys had ridden Burrough Hill Lad. Phil Tuck did a great job but wasn't always available. Becoming accustomed to different riding styles was part of the learning experience for a horse. During his novice years, various riders had all brought something extra to the party. Now Stan wanted to step things up a gear and thought it was time for consistency, so he sought out the best man for the job. One name kept cropping up: Johnny Francome.

The son of a railway fireman, John Francome's parents hoped early on that he would become a vet, but after a donkey ride during a holiday at Barry Island, the young boy's future was fixed. Johnny's mum and dad scrimped to buy him a milkman's pony, Black Beauty, for £50. Young John admired show jumpers David Broome and Harvey Smith, which led to a passion for the sport, but after scraping through school he had a sudden change of heart and decided the big money lay in racing. Johnny went on to apprentice for Fred Winter and won his first National Hunt Championship in 1976, aged 24. He had everything necessary for success; talent, grit, an insatiable desire to win and luck.

Stan told Jenny this was the man for him and she invited Johnny over. However, things didn't get off to the best start. During the first practice session at Lambourn, groom Scobie Jones was asked to fetch Burrough Hill Lad in order for John to school him. 'Jenny made John Francome stand there and watch me ride him round the bowl. She wouldn't let him on because she said Burrough Hill

Lad's legs were too dicky and he'd go too fast. As I always looked after him, she made the Champion Jockey stand there and watch me ride him.'

When Johnny eventually jumped on, he rode the horse with consummate ease until the final fence when he took a surprising tumble. Burrough Hill Lad was a little erratic when approaching hurdles, hardly surprising given the significant lay-off since his last race, and it was a lesson Jenny was keen for Johnny to learn.

Johnny said, 'He had a reputation for not being a very good jumper and Jenny said, "Get on and see what you think." But he was a great horse; a fantastic ride; a really good horse to sit on, big and strong. Some horses are big and they feel weak, he didn't. When you sat on him you felt as if you could jump anything and do anything. He was a proper horse.'

Johnny had great respect for Jenny and if she wanted something done, he was more than happy to try. 'She knew the horses inside out, she saw them every day. The reason she ended up being such a good trainer was she didn't miss anything. She used to sit and watch them all day long and knew their ailments and what was going on in their heads – that's what made her a good trainer. She wasn't interested in doing anything else. That was her whole life, horses.'

Midway through the previous season, Burrough Hill Lad had finished with a show – the result of a badly strained ligament that caused thickening. He'd come second to Silver Buck in the Edward Hanmer Memorial Chase at Haydock on 24 November 1982, a highly respectable and remarkable result considering his injury. There was no question Burrough Hill Lad needed the ligament sorting to have any chance of successfully racing again.

Despite controversy surrounding the procedure, Jenny recommended Burrough Hill Lad's leg be line-fired, even though it meant he would be unable to race for a year.

Opponents to the ancient practice considered it cruel, others swore by its efficacy. The hair around the leg is clipped and the horse is sedated before a local anaesthetic applied. Then a red-hot firing iron is placed against the lower leg. The iron burns lines around the leg or is pressed into the leg to penetrate the tendon.

It's assumed this stimulates the old injury and creates scar tissue to strengthen the tendons. However, the healing process took months and Stan was warned Burrough Hill Lad could be out of action for up to a year. Opponents of firing were convinced that time alone cured the injury, not the invasive and painful procedure. During the slow recovery process, great care had to be taken about not to exert too much pressure on Buzby's tendon while his leg healed.

Scobie Jones had no doubt Burrough Hill Lad needed the procedure. 'If he hadn't been fired he'd have never seen a race course. I know a lot of people don't agree with it but when Jenny Pitman first started she had many of them bar-fired. The night before you clip all the hair off. You get powdered mustard and a bit of water, mix it together then you rub it in like mad. In the morning the leg is full of fluid, like an elephant's leg. They put the red hot iron over the top of that. The tendon has very little blood in it. What you're doing is increasing the blood supply.'

Despite looking good in training, an air of trepidation surrounded Burrough Hill Lad when he reappeared for a warm-up race on 10 December 1983 at Nottingham over two and three-quarter miles. This was to be his first competition for almost thirteen months. Stan felt nervous walking towards the paddock. The past year had dragged by and he missed the sight and sounds of the track. Still, if Buzby was back at his best it would be worth it. Stan steadfastly refused to contemplate life without Burrough Hill Lad. It was all about the here and now, tomorrow was of no consequence and worrying about the future would only give him ulcers.

Whether it was the line-firing procedure or the en-forced rest, Burrough Hill Lad ended the race like a train in third place. He was back – with an extra turn of speed. Stan went home vindicated and a very happy man.

Just a couple of weeks later, the day after Boxing Day, Burrough Hill Lad was favourite at 100/30 in the Coral Welsh National at Chepstow. A dank drizzly day, it had been raining almost non-stop for the past week, making the going really heavy. Not that Burrough Hill Lad no-ticed. He plodded round the parade ring like he was half asleep.

Jenny Pitman had issued strict dietary orders to John Francome ahead of the festivities. 'I told John not to have too much Christmas pudding to do the lowest weight on the Lad – and he only put up an extra three.'

The jockey's abstinence paid off and it proved to be a smooth ride. Johnny cast aside any festive rustiness and was in untouchable form, beating Royal Judgement by four lengths. Jenny couldn't have been more pleased with such an easy victory. 'John had him jumping off his hocks and we never had an anxious moment.' She joked, 'All John needs now is a barrow to get his presents home. I wish I had the courage to back him when he was at 20/1.'

Stan at first was a little more guarded, always awkward about being quoted in the national press. 'He's an extremely good jockey and I wouldn't have minded another pound or two,' he said stiffly. Then, perhaps caught up in the jovial atmosphere of the festive season, Stan threw caution to the wind and publicly declared a desire for greater things. 'I think we could go for the Cheltenham Gold Cup.' It was a controversial statement aimed at the doubters who didn't feel Buzby was up to it. Stan had laid down the gauntlet.

Now the issue would not go away. Did Burrough Hill Lad have the class to step up to the big one?

One thing was undeniable. Jenny had won the Coral Welsh National two years running with horses that had previously been badly crocked. If there remained criticism of her controversial treatment, she believed this was proof positive her actions were justified. 'But for the line firing operations they would have been standing around in a field or sent to a knacker's yard,' she claimed.

1984 dawned, the year George Orwell immortalized in his dystopian novel. Burrough Hill Lad came in as the favourite at Sandown for the Andrew Mildmay, Peter Cazlet Memorial Handicap Chase. This time Corbiere fell at the sixteenth with Burrough Hill Lad going on to win so easily it was like he was running on his own. It was coming together beautifully. 'The only problem,' Jenny Pitman said wryly, 'was pulling him up afterwards. Johnny Francome says he has never known a horse accelerate so quickly.'

In early February, with the Gainsborough Chase fast approaching, a mystery bug swept through Jenny's stable. No one knew its origins and there was no cure. Several of her horses had been laid low and it appeared to be affecting their stamina.

'Five of my horses have all stopped suddenly in the last half mile after having winning chances. It's a virus of some sort that doesn't even show on the blood test until they have run,' she explained.

Thankfully, luck was on Burrough Hill Lad's side and he escaped unscathed. He raced well, apart from a mad moment when he veered sharply to the left approaching the last fence. The sight of photographers' flashbulbs suddenly lighting up made Stan grab his binoculars to get a better look. To his relief, Burrough Hill Lad steadied himself for the last and took it in his stride, romping home yet again.

What took punters by surprise was the performance of the 7/4 favourite Silver Buck. He faded right off the pace and trailed off into last place. Trainer Michael Dickinson refused to be drawn on how good a winner Burrough Hill Lad was, too busy lamenting his own horse's failure. 'Silver Buck has a temperature and is feeling a bit poorly. I do not know what is wrong with him.' In all probability the same virus that hit Jenny's stable was to blame for this horse's lacklustre performance.

Accolades for Burrough Hill Lad came thick and fast, and with them the odds to win the Gold Cup were cut from 10/1 to 6/1.

Burrough Hill Lad wasn't the only one receiving plaudits. It was a nice surprise when a panel of racing journalists crowned Jenny January's Piper Champagne Trainer of the Month. 'That's the best news I've had all week,' she smiled.

Yet despite all the acclaim, surprisingly things weren't going quite as smoothly for Stan. The knives were out. Punters couldn't understand what he was up to and questioned his sense of loyalty. Phil Tuck was once again demoted in favour of John Francome. Whilst Phil may not have been as famous as Johnny, he had a legion of fans and was a good steady rider. He also knew Burrough Hill Lad better than most as he'd been with him from the start. So why on earth, they asked, wasn't he in the saddle?

Stan failed to see what all the fuss was about and kept his own counsel. He wanted the best chance of winning and didn't see why he should have to explain anything.

Phil also refused to be drawn. He let others do the talking, only later admitting with usual frankness he didn't see the problem. 'I was riding Lasobany in the Welsh National for Harry Bell and Francome was riding Burrough Hill Lad. He won and kept the ride.' He would have expected nothing else.

However, with the truth getting in the way of a good story the conspiracy theorists refused to accept the most obvious explanation and the debate raged on. It sold newspapers.

Keen to dampen speculation, Stan came out of the shadows and put pen to paper. He wrote a fulsome note to the local paper and set the record straight. 'I have always thought a lot of Phil Tuck and always will. I can honestly say my phone was a hotline the Sunday before the Welsh National trying to get Phil to ride Burrough, but as he could not give us a definite yes or no, I could not afford to lose John Francome. Any reasonable-minded human being can understand the predicament both of us were in. Phil not only earns his bread and butter but also his jam riding for the majority of the northern trainers and we cannot be a part of taking away what he has worked so hard for.'

Stan added one slightly contentious note, 'We do think however, it would have been honourable of Harry Bell to have let Phil have the ride he was most certain of winning on, knowing Burrough so well.' He signed off saying, 'In future when referring to my horse please note he is not a machine, he is my own bred horse of which I am very proud.'

Rather than end the issue, it only fanned the fire. Whispers circulated that John Francome had other commitments and would be unavailable to ride Burrough Hill Lad for the Gold Cup. The back pages were now busy predicting the jockey would be either Ben de Haan or, in a volte-face, Phil Tuck.

Johnny found it all rather intriguing. 'There was never a question I was going to ride Burrough Hill Lad in the Gold Cup,' he said. 'I'd ridden for Fred Winter since I left school. He had a runner called Brown Chamberlin in the race and I was never going to ask to get off him. Also Brown Chamberlin was owned by Coral Samuel who'd been really loyal to me. I was retained to ride for one stable and that's what I did. You look after the people who look after you.'

While the brouhaha over Gold Cup jockeys raged on, Burrough Hill Lad had a further outing back at Wincanton for the Jim Ford Challenge over three miles one furlong. Waiting there for him was the magnificent Bregawn, Cheltenham Gold Cup winner the previous year, when Michael Dickinson walked into the history books by training the first five finishers. Now that Burrough Hill Lad was coming into the form of his life, it promised to be a true clash of the titans.

It was an extraordinary race with Bregawn leading from the start, seemingly in magnificent form. Yet by the fourteenth it was quite a different story and only a superhuman effort from jockey Graham Bradley got the horse over. At the next, he dug his heels in, stopped on the spot and simply refused to go one step further. Despite Brad-ley's best efforts, there was no way he could even attempt a take off. 'He was going as sweet as a nut until then,' said the bemused jockey, unable to account for Bregawn's behaviour.

Until that point the pair had been galloping in tandem but Burrough Hill Lad was so busy watching Bregawn he almost stopped alongside and followed suit. Fortunately, a quick kick from John Francome got his act together in time to win his fourth race in a row, to rapturous ap-plause. Afterwards Jenny Pitman effused, 'I am very con-fident about Cheltenham, and he had an easy race today.' Stan was elated. Burrough Hill Lad might as well have been out on a training run, it was that effortless.

Unfortunately the good news didn't last long. After all the controversy, it was full circle for Phil Tuck. Jenny and Stan agreed he was the man to ride Burrough Hill Lad at Cheltenham. However, with less than three weeks to go, luck was not on Phil's side and he had a bad fall on Welfare at Sedgefield, taking a smash full in the face and breaking his nose. Although Phil hadn't ridden Burrough Hill Lad for nearly a year and half, he was widely credited with the horse's early success and Jenny still wanted him back in the saddle. Now there seemed little chance of him recovering in time. His injuries were extensive and if he fell again the worry was any damage may be irreversible.

Wanting to give Phil every chance, Jenny pencilled him in as the most likely to ride and crossed her fingers. She even saw the funny side when a heavily bandaged

Phil wandered around doing impressions of Darth Vader. Huge white plasters covered his forehead, cheeks and newly straightened nose and Phil thought a bit of good humour would aid his recovery. It certainly broke the tension. Stoic as ever, Phil refuted any suggestion he may not be ready. 'I don't care what I look like as long as I'm fit for Cheltenham,' he said. Just as well.

Teflon Phil refused to let any injury stick. The Gold Cup would be the pinnacle of his career and whatever it took, he would be there. Being hurt was just part and parcel of riding at such an intense level. 'I never worried about it,' he said. 'If I had I would never have got on the horse. People say you're brave, but to be honest it was a job same as anyone else. It just happened to be my job to ride a horse over steeplechase fences and hurdles and I loved every minute of if. But I couldn't give getting injured a thought.'

Phil had already notched up more than his fair share of pain and suffering, including a broken foot, dislocated shoulder and a smashed back to go with his now badly-broken nose. Perhaps it was no surprise that he became highly superstitious, devising a set of lucky rituals from saluting magpies to wearing the same tatty socks each race. 'I filled the medical record book during my time,' said Phil, 'and it didn't look as if I'd get back in time for the Gold Cup.' Fortunately, he defied doctors' predictions.

Having won his last four races, Burrough Hill Lad was, for some, too good to be true. They didn't trust his ability and speculation about his fitness the week before the Gold Cup swept along the grapevine. Rumours, apparently phoned in by a 'good source', speculated the horse had burst blood vessels. While the racing fraternity has always existed on nods and winks, this went beyond the usual conjecture about form. It had a distinctly malevolent intent. Jenny Pitman almost blew a gasket. Whatever she said made absolutely no difference. Betting on the Lad inevitably took a tumble. Stan had a unique take on the situation – if people wanted to think Burrough Hill Lad was injured, they must believe he could win.

He saw it as a strangely good omen.

10

There is nothing quite like the Gold Cup. One of the most spectacular events in the racing calendar, it attracts big money and has earned a special place in sporting history.

The first race took place in July 1819 on Cleeve Hill and was won by Spectre, earning prize money of 100 guineas. Back then it was on the flat, only much later in 1924 did it become a jump festival. Sixty years on, in 1984, it was well established as the blue riband event at Cheltenham.

Thousands flocked from all around the country to watch the three mile, two and a half furlong race over

22 fences and major money changed hands amidst a sea of champagne. It was, unashamedly, the one that every owner longed to win.

Jenny Pitman woke early on 15 March 1984, sick with worry. She had long ago confessed that, on race days, 'I'm terrible.' Today, she could barely eat and watched Burrough Hill Lad like a hawk. What if he gets injured? What if they are late? What if something happens to him?

It had been building for a while. On the day of his last race at Wincanton, she lost four pounds in weight beforehand from fretting. Her father George calmed her down with a few kind words. 'She was so full of it, she was flying. I thought we'd be calling an ambulance and she was going to have a breakdown.'

Jenny had every right to be concerned. These were troubled times. Dropping your guard could lead to all sorts of problems. Fears had surfaced about a new nasal drug which was being used by unscrupulous gangs to get at horses. The drug was very hard to detect, quick acting and would affect a horse only after they had run some distance. The police were involved following allegations that these gangs had nobbled horses in a betting fraud.

Still just a year since Shergar's kidnap and on police advice, Jenny had enhanced security by installing £1500 worth of cameras in both Corbiere and Burrough Hill Lad's boxes. She even placed the monitor in her bedroom so she could keep an eye on them while she was in bed. As if that weren't enough, she requested that groom Andrew Scobie Jones sleep in Burrough Hill Lad's box. Assistant trainer David Strait, later to become Jenny's second husband, went public about the special measures in the hope of warding off potential threats.

Scobie Jones didn't take Jenny as literally as she would have liked. Bedding down with a horse was hardly his idea of a good night's sleep. 'I was actually sleeping in the tack room right next to his box,' he said. But he did spend many a night wondering what would happen if a criminal sneaked into the yard. 'Someone turns up with a shotgun and I've got a pitchfork, what am I going to do? Stick it down the barrel?'

Thankfully he was never put to the test, although he admitted he would go to extraordinary lengths for Burrough Hill Lad. 'I really believed in him, I'd have done anything for that horse. I loved him, full belt. I was single and that was the nearest thing I've had to being married!'

Probably the only one of the team who slept well that Gold Cup eve was Burrough Hill Lad. Up at 6 o'clock for an early morning run to get the adrenalin pumping and muscles warmed, he was back for a half bowl of oats before leaving Lambourn on the 45 mile journey to Cheltenham. Jenny wanted Burrough Hill Lad settled and ready well before the race.

Scobie Jones was under orders to keep things as normal as possible. 'It was just another race day,' he said. 'I mucked him out, rode out with my first lot, came back, got him ready to travel, bandaged him up and then it was off. I sat outside his box because everybody was still very nervous about doping and other things going on. So me and the travel head lad, Steve Fox, took it in turns. I'd go to the canteen to have something to eat and Steve would stand there till I came back.'

Scobie Jones' final job was to put the finishing touches to Burrough Hill Lad's mane, brushing his coat until it shone like glass. Today of all days the horse had to look his very best and besides, Scobie had his reputation to uphold.

'I always plaited his mane and tail and we won every "best turned out" he was ever in, bar the Hennessy. That day he had top weight so we saddled him very late and didn't actually get into the paddock, we just did one circuit and out.'

As for jockey Phil Tuck, despite a cool exterior, this was the day when all his bizarre rituals really kicked in. If things got intense, there was no stopping him. 'I was terrible. I even named my house in Yorkshire "The Magpies" and painted it black and white. The day my wife Maria and I travelled from Stratford to the races, we saw two magpies and sat in silence for about twenty minutes before seeing another two, which meant four for a boy! I suppose it could have easily been six for gold as the rhyme goes.'

When he arrived at Cheltenham he followed a well established routine. 'I had to wear the same sweater that my mother knitted and it was more darn than sweater. The elastic bands on my wrists would be used until they snapped, same as the safety pin to fasten the colours' collar. I put on my right sock and boot first. The tights I wore under breeches had to be worn by my wife before I used them. I also wore her hair bands on my wrists plus several Saint Christopher medals around my neck.'

It was just another normal day at work for Phil. Stan also refused to make a fuss. To keep the nerves at bay he stuck to his routine too, albeit one much less involved than Phil Tuck's. Sue remembers, 'Dad slept well at home the night before, at least better than Kath! He had his usual full English for breakfast and they got dressed and ready. He wore his normal "good" race day clothes – grey suit, white shirt and tie with his almost-new sheepskin coat over the top. He'd bought the coat from a shop in Ashby de la Zouch for about £160. Not only were sheepskin coats practical for keeping the cold out at the races but they were very on trend in those days.'

Oddly, and for a reason Stan still can't fathom, he made a small but significant change to his dress. Normally he would wear his trilby hat. 'But not today,' said Sue.

Stan nonchalantly strung his binoculars round his neck, numerous badges dangling like medals from the straps. He checked his goatee beard, flattened his thick mop of unruly hair with the back of his hand and then it was time to leave for the two hour drive to Cheltenham. Just as he jumped in the van, he realised the horse racing bible, the *Racing Post*, hadn't been delivered. Today of all days! So Stan set off desperately trying to find the paper boy. 'I spotted him further up the village,' said Stan, 'and grabbed the paper off him. The paper boy had no idea why I was so keen to have his paper that day!'

When they arrived at the course, Stan did some tough negotiation with the taciturn parking attendant who refused them entry. 'You can't come in, not in that van,' he said snootily. Kath turned on the charm and persuaded him they really did have the inside track on which horse would win the Gold Cup. Kath kept smiling and said she was willing to wager a few quid of her own money on the suspicious parking attendant's behalf. And if she won, he was welcome to the winnings. At that the man managed a smile and waved them in. Once inside, Stan stayed well away from Burrough Hill Lad. Over time he had become a little more superstitious and felt it could bring bad luck if he talked to him before a race. Anyway, he didn't want to be accused of causing Burrough Hill Lad to lose focus. On occasion, one of Jenny's lads would call over and encourage Stan to the box. But he learned not to mess with fate. Some things you can't explain. If Burrough Hill Lad ran better without seeing Stan, why change routine at a time like this?

Stan left the final preparations to Jenny. She knew how to keep Burrough Hill Lad calm and get the best from him. 'I hadn't arranged to meet with Jenny beforehand,' Stan said, 'we would see each other about half an hour before the race near the parade ring. Before then Jenny would be busy checking all Burrough Hill Lad's tack. She was always very thorough and took personal responsibility for everything.'

Stan waited patiently to ask the one question on his mind. 'How is he today?'

Jenny calmly answered, 'He's fine Stan. He's looking well.'

Scobie Jones knew Burrough Hill Lad may have been about to ride the race of his life but no one would guess from seeing him before the start.

'He never looked much until he got on the parade ring and then he pumped himself up. It was the same when you were walking down to the gallops on him, you wouldn't think a lot about him until he was within about 200 yards of the gallops and then he'd just literally blow up underneath you. His shoulders and neck would come out, he'd tuck himself in and he was a monster then. He loved winning, that's what he loved doing.'

As Stan strode back to the stand he knew he could do nothing more. Then the importance of the day really hit home. 'It was a surreal situation,' said Stan. 'Was I really having one of my horses run in the most prestigious National Hunt race there is? With every chance of winning?'

Burrough Hill Lad left the parade ring to make his way down to the start. Stan meanwhile had a sudden attack of stomach cramp and ran to find the nearest lavatory. 'It was the nerves,' said Sue. 'It always happened at big races.'

Sue dashed to the Owners and Trainers Stand where Jenny waited anxiously with her mum and dad. Soon Kath joined her and, a few moments later, a pale-looking Stan. Kath stood next to Mary Harvey, Jenny Pitman's mother, and chatted away, just like they always did. They were race buddies, offering each other female company in this man's world. Their easy friendship helped settle Kath's nerves – she was trying hard to keep calm for Stan, now pacing around the stand. Kath more than anyone knew just how much this moment meant to him and the sacrifice it had taken to make it happen.

Back in Burrough, the 'closed' sign had mysteriously appeared on the post office door. Stan told Angela in no uncertain terms that some things are more important than stamps. Burrough Hill Lad needed all the support he could get.

'Lock the post office door Ange,' Stan said, 'watch the race on the TV upstairs, and if he wins I'll treat you and your mum to a new winter coat.'

Luckily for Angela, you could hear a pin drop in the lanes round Burrough that afternoon. Nobody was the slightest bit interested in buying stamps. The whole village was glued to the BBC, sets on full volume so as not to miss a thing.

Further down Main Street, Ena and Bill Fryer caught a first glimpse of Phil Tuck in the colours Ena once knitted. 'I'm not a racing man,' said Bill, 'but everyone was very excited.' This horse had put their tiny village on the map.

The crowd poured through Cheltenham's turnstiles, 38,477 paying customers from all round the country. Sue tried to take it all in and at that moment reflected, 'Most people in racing are very wealthy but Dad was just a poor tenant farmer. His horses were that important to him he went without other things to keep them. Some people thought he was tight. But if you haven't got the money, there's not much you can do about it. If you haven't got it, you haven't got it. But all the money in the world couldn't buy what Dad had that day with Burrough Hill Lad.'

Last minutes instructions were being issued to Phil Tuck in the paddock. 'Jenny said to me "don't get beat" and how could I disobey her? This was the first time I was riding for her. She was a great woman and a great trainer, very fair, and very good with me.'

It was time. The twelve runners were under starter's orders and Stan's heart had never beaten so fast.

From the off, Brown Chamberlin took the lead round the left handed course, just a short head in front of Bregawn. The normally reliable Wayward Lad hit the second ditch hard, almost unseating jockey Robert Earnshaw. From then on, he struggled to get back in contention. The pack moved steadily until six from home when Brown Chamberlin edged ahead of both Burrough Hill Lad and Wayward Lad. Turning down the back straight on the final circuit, Bregawn dropped away while the leader Brown Chamberlin continued to move strongly. The pace got steadily faster and Burrough Hill Lad duly responded, lengthening his long stride.

The field started to spread as the main contenders pushed on, jostling for position. The number 4 on Burrough Hill Lad's flank flapped in the wind as he manoeuvred alongside Brown Chamberlin, Scot Lane, Drumlargan and Canny Danny.

Down the hill at the seventeenth, Burrough Hill Lad moved steadily into second place behind Brown Chamberlin and the cheers from the stand reached the track.

Breathless and excited, willing their horse on; Stan, Kath and Sue stood united during these last tense moments.

Suddenly it was a three horse race – John Francome burst forward on Brown Chamberlin with Burrough Hill Lad close behind. Drumlargan was working flat out just to keep up and it now appeared his only chance lay in both of his opponents making a mistake.

Then there were two.

Over the last, Francome incomprehensibly began to drift to the right. Here was Burrough Hill Lad's opportunity. Keeping a good line, he lengthened his stride yet again and moved up another gear. Phil eyed the shortest route to the finish line and kept him straight as a die. The post was within touching distance. While Johnny veered over to the right-hand rails, Phil pushed Burrough Hill Lad on and he responded beautifully, each stride edging him ever closer. They were almost there.

Then there was a thunderous roar. Burrough Hill Lad slowed to a canter and looked around, as if acknowledging what had just happened.

He had won the Gold Cup!

Phil punched the air and leaned forward to give Burrough Hill Lad one mighty 'good boy' slap on the side. They'd done it! 'Words can't describe how I feel,' said Phil soon after. 'This is the happiest day of my life.'

Their strategy worked perfectly. 'We always wanted to be reasonably handy, which is pretty well how the race unfolded,' said Phil. 'Bregawn was mulish leaving the stands on the second circuit, which gave me the chance to move up to third behind Brown Chamberlin. Bregawn came back upside jumping the water but I was going really well. From about six fences out I could see that Wayward Lad was beaten. Mrs P said "make sure you jump the third last" and once over I could see Brown Chamberlin edging out to his right so was able to get up the inside. Once we turned into the straight it was pretty much all over.'

Stan was in a state of shock. As he made his way to the enclosure everything seemed to slow down. The crowd surged, cocooning him in victory.

Back in Burrough, Angela jumped up and waved her arms in celebration, landing so hard on the wooden floor she knocked Kath's precious cups flying out of the china cabinet. Despite the chaos she managed to spot Phil Tuck on TV raising his arm in salute. It was really true. Burrough Hill Lad was a champion!

Angela had no qualms about reopening the shop after such a wonderful victory. It was a pleasure being able to chat with customers and share the historic moment. Angela wore the biggest smile in Burrough all day long.

In Cheltenham, Phil was congratulated by his fellow jockeys, even his fiercest competitors sportingly giving the thumbs up. Rivalry fades pretty quickly once over the finish line.

The only disappointment was that Phil had committed to riding again and had to delay his celebration. 'I went back into the weighing room and sent out for champagne which was given out to anyone in the room, but later I was in the County Hurdle so had to wait until after that before joining my family. The camaraderie was terrific,' he remembers, adding, 'although it took Johnny Francome about an hour to say well done to me.'

Phil will never forget what happened next. 'There is a tradition that the horse's name is written above the rider's changing peg and then signed by the jockey. I was a DIY jockey so I didn't employ a valet. However, one of the northern valets wrote on the wall, but spelled Burrough Hill Lad's name wrong!'

John Francome later admitted, 'When I was out there for the seven minutes or however long the race took, all I wanted to do was beat him, but as soon as you're beaten you're pleased for him. That was it. It was nice to see it and good for him. But I wasn't shocked, I thought Burrough Hill Lad was well up for winning the Gold Cup.'

Stan was on cloud nine. 'At the last fence he was so close,' said Stan. 'And for a split second it crossed my mind that it would just be my luck to get pipped going across the line. The crowds were cheering loudly and it was so noisy. We just wanted Burrough Hill Lad to get round and come home safely, and negotiate all the fences without injury. Once he cleared the last we could let out our breath.'

It was only as they galloped the last few strides for home that Stan started to celebrate. He could see his life's dream about to come true. 'It was unbelievable,' said Stan. 'We really enjoyed his triumphant run to the line.'

Stan gripped onto Kath's hand as they were ushered towards the winner's enclosure. He was struggling to find the right words, any words, to sum up the last twenty minutes. 'I was in complete disbelief, almost overwhelmed. It felt like a dream.' As they approached the enclosure, course officials guided them through. But Sue was nowhere to be seen. Separated in the aftermath of victory, the crowd now blocked her exit and she was stranded, left behind, all alone in the stand.

Marooned away from her family, Sue jumped frantically up and down, desperately trying to catch sight of her dad. On the verge of giving up, she received help from a most unexpected source. 'This fella, who was a blacksmith, knew who I was and dragged me through the crowd yelling, "Winning owner's daughter! Winning owner's daughter!" ' He refused to take no for an answer and led Sue all the way to the paddock. 'If it hadn't been for him I'd never have got through,' she said.

Meanwhile, head lad Scobie Jones was trying to lead Burrough Hill Lad through the crowds. 'I'd been watching the race in the Lads Stand, which is about 100 yards before the post. I thought he'd win it. But Fred Winter's horse was coming up the rail on the stand side and all Fred Winter's lads went "Yes!" and ran up the track and I thought, shit, we're beat. Then all of a sudden they gave out the result and I tell you what, I went up that track quicker than Ben Johnson. My dad was there and he said, "I have to get into the winner's enclosure to see my boy," and there were two big coppers, and he's only a short arse, pointing at me going, "That's my boy! That's my boy! I've got to go and see my boy." These two big six foot coppers said, "Shall we let him? Yeah alright then." My dad then got through as well. It was one of the best days of his life! The atmosphere was absolutely manic. I was leading Burrough Hill Lad in through a crowd of about a thousand people hanging on the breast girth and Phil Tuck was riding him. We were just dragged through the crowd.'

Stan walked over and congratulated Phil Tuck before he dismounted and disappeared into the weighing room. 'What a fantastic day,' said Phil. Journalists and cameramen dashed forward eager for Jenny's reaction, now the first woman to train a Gold Cup winner. 'How do you feel?' they yelled. While Stan stood quietly amongst the melee, Jenny gathered herself. It was important people understood things exactly as they were. 'It's a big race and if you win this race your horse is a champion,' she smiled. 'This year it was an intriguing race and nobody knew what was going to happen. There had been rumours about Burrough Hill Lad and they were totally unfounded and it made the race even more important as I wanted to prove to people I'd been telling the truth. There is nothing wrong with the horse and when they came down the hill, I was very, very happy because I knew he had another gear. Nobody has seen his top gear this year, as he's never had to produce it! Once he hit the second last he absolutely flew and I'm very proud of him. Phil rode him marvellously. He nipped up Johnny's inner round the last bend and there's not many that get up Johnny's inner. He followed my instructions out, but I obviously told him to make up his own mind if things go wrong. I love the jumpers, they are the men of this sport. It's my privilege to train him.'

To resounding applause, Jenny retreated to check all was well with Burrough Hill Lad. Making no exceptions for this or any other race, she did as always and bandaged his legs. She made sure he recovered as well as he could after such a mammoth victory.

'What's going to happen now?' came the cry when she returned to the paddock.

'He won't run again this year as he's only eight, and still a baby, and he's done enough,' Jenny sighed. 'He's improved out of all recognition. He's a real athlete with a bit of extra class. The only sad part is that I'm not a gambler or otherwise I'd be having a holiday in Barbados.'

As the moment arrived for Stan to meet the Queen Mother, he didn't know where to put himself. From the generation that greatly admired the most senior Royal for her common touch during wartime, she epitomised everything that was stoic and great about the country. Stan, who had started life as a poor tenant farmer, was about to shake hands with royalty. That change in circumstance was due to hard work, grit and a little bit of luck; nevertheless he remained a shy man. He may have bred a Gold Cup winner but was petrified of the tiny Queen Mother.

'I had no idea what I was going to say,' Stan said. He smiled nervously at Kath who whispered, 'Just be yourself,' then made his way to the Royal Box. Legs like jelly, he climbed the steps, certain everyone could hear his heart pounding in his chest.

The Queen Mother instantly recognised his awkward-ness and moved forward with a big smile to put him at ease. 'There were lots of press photographers pushing and shoving to get pictures as the Queen Mum appeared from the Royal Box to present the trophy,' recalls Sue. 'I was ob-viously in the wrong place again, because I got squashed and trodden on by them. After the presentation, Dad and Kath were invited by a royal official up to the Royal Box for a drink along with Jenny and her mum and dad. The official looked me up and down and then decided against it, so I wasn't invited. I like to tell myself it was because I wasn't wearing a hat! Dad didn't even know where he was by then, so I was left standing there on my own for a few moments until rescued by my delighted boyfriend.'

Stan held out his trembling hand towards the Queen Mother to take the coveted Gold Cup. 'She told me her daughter, the Queen, had sent a mare to Barley Thorpe for stud,' said Stan. 'Then she asked me what it was like to win a big race. She had 327 wins but had never won a race as big as this. She was very kind and charming and said she hoped to see me next year.'

'Dad was smitten,' said Sue. 'The Queen Mum chatted to him like an old friend.'

Stan came away walking on air. He didn't want to let the Gold Cup go – it was, after all, one of horse racing's most iconic trophies. And he'd managed to conduct a conversation with the Queen Mother! As he left, he said it was the difference between them that had made him feel nervous – not the difference in social class, but in stature – he towered above her and had to stoop down to hear. 'She was so small, I thought she'd have a bit more height about her.'

It had been a long day and when Jenny suggested fish and chips back at her place, everyone agreed that was a lovely way to round off the celebrations.

There was just one more thing Kath had to do before they left. She searched out the parking attendant and handed him the winnings, plus her stake. He was so pleased he gave them the red carpet treatment on the way out.

As Scobie Jones drove away, horns and cheers resounded around the car park. 'There was a Capri with a sun roof and the passengers asked, "Who have you got in there?" and I said, "Burrough Hill Lad." They shouted, "We backed him. Brilliant!" They handed us a bottle of champagne but didn't realise there were six of us so we all had a swig and handed them back an empty bottle!'

Sue vividly remembers the journey back to Lambourn. 'Jenny invited us back to hers at Weathercock House. She preferred to get back home and make sure the horses were all safe and sound rather than go out celebrating. I travelled with Dad and Kath in the campervan and on the way we listened to the racing results on the radio, Burrough Hill Lad's win still not quite sinking in. We were all exhausted.'

Luckily the campervan meant Stan, Kath and Sue could bed down as soon as the celebrations started to wane, and in the wee small hours they didn't have far to go.

'Dad parked right next to the yard and that's where the three of us slept that Gold Cup night.'

The whole day had been a blur and Sue was just glad their much loved horse was still in one piece. 'The night before the Gold Cup I was praying, I don't care where Burrough Hill Lad finishes, just please let him come home safely. Like Dad, I don't think I ever considered that he might actually win it, even though he was one of the top favourites with the bookies. To be honest it was somewhat of a relief when it all came to an end. Although very exciting, it was quite stressful being under the spotlight. At least Burrough Hill Lad was alive and okay and nothing fatally tragic had happened on a racecourse that made headlines in the papers the next day. Like Dad, I didn't much like the attention.'

Meanwhile Jenny's staff partied the night away. 'We went back to Jenny's after the racing,' Scobie Jones said. 'Then we went to the Malt Shovel, then we went to the Red Lion, then we had a party in my house. There were a few who didn't make it in the morning. And there were a few girls who worked for Jenny who were asleep under the table in her house.'

The next morning, after Stan said his goodbyes to Burrough Hill Lad, Jenny and all the team, they set off back home. 'On the way we stopped for lunch in a service station and picked up a couple of newspapers,' said Stan. 'I said that I needed to see it in black and white to make sure it was true and I wasn't still dreaming!'

In Leicestershire, Stan went round to Angela's and handed her an envelope. Inside was enough money to buy good winter coats for her and her mum.

11

It was time to celebrate the Gold Cup victory.

Stan still couldn't quite believe what had happened until a few days later, when the winner's cheque dropped through his letter box. Stan stared at his name and the instruction to 'Pay the bearer the sum of £66,000'. Then he drove to Anstey, where the now friendly bank manager dashed out to offer his heartfelt congratulations.

Stan settled Jenny's training bills and set aside money for Burrough Hill Lad's further upkeep. Then, following a chat with Kath, he drove down to the Mercedes garage. Looking for a little luxury, Stan decided to upgrade the campervan.

After withdrawing £12,000 from his account, he pointed to a top of the range, brand new, red and white Mercedes 307 motorhome complete with cooker, fridge and indoor toilet. It was a long way from the days they had camped in the estate car on a blow-up bed.

Stan wanted to make life for Kath a little easier and this was a way to show he loved her. She still tired easily and was under the care of a cardiologist who had been urging her to undergo a replacement heart valve operation. The surgery frightened Kath so she resolved to deal with her illness her own way, trusting that the medication and a dose of denial would see her through.

The new motorhome turned out to be an absolute treasure and great distraction from their worries. They could travel in style and stay overnight, stretched out in a comfortable bed with a heater to keep them warm whenever it was chilly.

There was another pressing matter on Stan's mind. He wasn't exactly being honest with Jenny. Their conversations had become rather clipped and forced. He was keeping something from her.

Exactly two weeks after Burrough Hill Lad's success, all was revealed when Jenny Pitman got the surprise of her career in the Theatre Royal on Drury Lane. She became the subject of the popular television series *This Is Your Life*.

The excitement leading up to the big reveal had been very hard to contain. 'A few weeks before the show, Dad received a phone call from a TV company explaining they wanted to do Jenny's life and inviting him and Kath to be guests,' said Sue. 'It was very top secret, tell no one, they said. On the day, Dad and Kath went along and when Jenny saw them, she thought they were at some sort of celebration dinner to do with Burrough Hill Lad and the Gold Cup! She was very surprised when she realized it was Eamonn Andrews and *This is Your Life.*'

Within the space of a fortnight, Stan had achieved the dream of his life time by winning the Gold Cup; met the Queen Mother and been interviewed on one of TV's most high rating programmes. 'I loved *This is Your Life,*' he said. 'I was glad when the secret was out, worried I might let something slip. Best of all was meeting up with Jenny's family and friends again.'

Mixing in circles he could only have dreamed of and with Burrough Hill Lad now centre stage, Stan's life had been turned upside down. No wonder then, over the next few months as the racing season drew to a close, Stan took a breather and turned his attention to other things. His new home was in need of modernisation. While Kath got busy behind the sewing machine making curtains and soft furnishings, Stan set about the garden creating a pond which he filled with exotic koi carp. After the tension of the race track it was a chance to go back to doing ordinary things and enjoying a slower pace of life.

They had four blissful weeks. Then their world exploded. Stan hit the headlines once more, for all the wrong reasons, this time not on the back pages.

At the age of 57, after a lifetime's self-employment and in the midst of a deep recession, his prospects for full-time work weren't great. In 1984, unemployment was the highest on record and the miners were on strike, locked in one of the longest and most damaging industrial disputes ever seen in Britain. These were hard times.

Around the time of the Gold Cup win, Stan had been earning a little cash from a series of part-time driving jobs. Soon even this piecemeal work dried up and Stan reluctantly went to the benefit office to sign on the dole.

Now a well-known face after all the Gold Cup publicity, someone most likely spotted him in the queue. The *Sun* newspaper got a call, did a bit of investigation and earmarked Stan's story for a front page splash. The shock death of comedian and national treasure, Tommy Cooper, was relegated to make way for news that Stan was claiming £27 a week in benefits.

The headline screamed, '£90,000 WINNER ON DOLE!' The story went on to report, 'Wealthy racehorse owner Stan Riley – winner of the Cheltenham Gold Cup – is drawing the dole. Mr Riley, whose steeplechaser Burrough Hill Lad won more than £90,000 this season, collects £27 a week from the state.' It said Stan had so much money he never needed to work again and was the proud owner of a smart bungalow, a car and a luxury caravanette.

It was a sensational front page. Back then there was no social media or means to set the record straight. Stan knew he had been portrayed in an unfair light yet had no choice but to tough it out.

The real story was much less dramatic. It was true he had won a lot of money, but his expenses were high. Over the years, debts had mounted which had to be repaid. He'd also endured 31 years as an owner without a win before Burrough Hill Lad's success so there were considerable losses to make up for. And while Burrough Hill Lad was with Jenny, the £91 weekly training fees had to be met, even if he wasn't racing, in addition to all the vet and blacksmith fees.

Jenny had long been of the opinion that steeplechasers were not the horses to own if you wanted to get rich. They were about the glory. 'Fifty thousand was probably what it cost to get Corbiere to Aintree,' she said, adding, 'Little wonder there's a racing adage which says that if you win the Derby it makes you rich, if you win the Grand National it makes you happy.'

Stan was savvy enough to understand that to the average person, his winnings seemed off the scale. Yet his path had been a high-risk strategy for a farmer's boy. Far from being born with a silver spoon in his mouth like some other horse owners, he had spent his life accounting for every last penny. To that end, Stan had no regrets about signing on, believing it his right as a taxpayer. He had worked hard and paid into the system. His frustration was with those who failed to understand what went on behind the racing scene, that it was not all gloss and glamour. Yes, he loved it, and without that passion he would have walked away. 'Of the prize money, ten per cent goes to the trainer and ten per cent goes to the jockey. The majority of what's left has to pay the horse's bills,' he said.

Most people were unaware that, just two years before, Stan was on the brink of bankruptcy from his ailing restaurant business. He had drawn up plans to sell Burrough Hill Lad, then at the last moment fended off his debtors by restructuring his finances. He confessed to a newspaper, 'Keeping a racehorse in training is a costly business and I could have done with the money at the time. But if I'd have sold him then, Burrough Hill Lad would have been the last racehorse in my life.' He took a massive gamble and fortunately it paid off. However, stories of a life of luxury were greatly exaggerated. Over time, Stan became more sanguine about the *Sun*'s story. Harking back to the supper after Burrough Hill Lad's Gold Cup win, he said, 'My front page ended up wrapped around someone's fish and chips. I did nothing wrong. I paid my dues.'

Sue said her dad had broad shoulders and wasn't one to dwell. 'It was water off a duck's back.' He had nothing to apologise for.

However, the stress did have an effect on Kath who began suffering dizzy spells and lapses in concentration. She kept it hidden from Stan, not wanting to add to his woes. She knew he would only worry.

Burrough Hill Lad didn't take to the track again until the end of the year in November at Cheltenham for the Standard Life Handicap Chase over three miles. After his success in the Gold Cup, it came as no surprise Phil Tuck was in the saddle. The summer lay off had not harmed Buzby's acceleration and speed, but like any top athlete he needed a few races under his belt to get into a good rhythm. Despite being 2/1 favourite and showing much of his old form, as he galloped towards the finish line he smacked into three barriers and lagged behind in third place. To some the performance was way below par. The stewards, aware of Burrough Hill Lad's usual capabilities, immediately began an inquiry.

The investigation centred on whether Phil Tuck refused to go for his whip and therefore failed to push Burrough Hill Lad hard enough. Jockey Club rules clearly stated 'schooling in public' was not allowed – in other words, trainers are forbidden to use any race as a practice run to get the horse's conditioning up to scratch. Jenny understood the stewards were only doing their job but refused to believe Phil Tuck hadn't given his best. 'Phil Tuck had strict instructions not to hit Burrough Hill Lad,' she confirmed. 'There was no point in giving him a hiding when he was not fully wound up. If Phil had thrashed the horse he may have finished two lengths closer.'

As the old saying goes; form is temporary, class is permanent. Six days later on 15 November, Burrough Hill Lad won comfortably at Wincanton. Stan, still unsettled by the steward's inquiry, was delighted that Buzby was back to winning ways. He'd always had a soft spot for John Francome and these latest events fostered his view someone of Francome's experience should be riding Burrough Hill Lad.

Unable to let the matter go, Stan requested Johnny be booked for the Hennessy Gold Cup on 24 November at Newbury. Jenny respected Stan's decision as the owner and reinstated Johnny. Sue too was more than happy. Francome's status as resident race heartthrob added a certain something. Johnny wasn't just handsome, his devil may care attitude lightened the mood in any camp. 'Johnny would say, "Come on everyone, stop looking so worried, we're here to win." He could break the tension and come out with all his long hair as if he didn't care. I really liked him because he'd always speak his mind.'

Before news of Phil Tuck's relegation hit the racing press, Jenny did the decent thing. 'She was excellent,' Phil said. 'She was good enough to ring me before I rode at Leicester. She said, "I want you to hear this from me. The owner wants Francome to ride Burrough Hill Lad in the Hennessy." I said, "OK – he who pays the piper, plays the tune." But I was disappointed.'

Whatever the future, Burrough Hill Lad held a very special place in Phil's heart. He could only speak well of him. 'He had a massive engine and was a relentless galloper but he could pick up as well. He's got to be the best horse I ever rode. He oozed quality and this big black horse had a real presence about him. He could stay all day.'

Phil eventually shrugged off rejection. He saw no point in holding a grudge and decided next time he saw Stan, he'd have a quiet word to clear the air. 'Although the news was buzzing round the press, I tried not to take too much notice,' said Phil. 'Shortly after I saw Stan Riley in the stands, walked up and said, "I'm very sorry you've reached the decision you've made. But I'm man enough to take it. I hope the horse runs well and I hope he wins for you. They can't take the Gold Cup from us. It was the highlight of my career."'

Stan explained his decision in straightforward terms. 'When the best becomes available you employ him. He'll be carrying less dead weight and he's worth ten pounds or more on the big occasion.'

Johnny, back in the saddle for the Hennessy Gold Cup, immediately had to contend with a mammoth twelve stone handicap. Seen by some as punishing and others as positively draconian, no horse had been asked to tolerate such extra weight since the glory days of Arkle.

However, the reunited partnership of Francome and Buzby sent a flurry of excitement throughout racing and was much discussed at the London Hilton that evening when Burrough Hill Lad won Outstanding Chaser at the Racehorse Owners Association dinner. Their odds as favourites for the Hennessy had already been clipped a point, to 3/1. With a day to go, Mecca and William Hill tightened the odds yet further to 11/4. Jenny remained circumspect. 'I have come to expect the odd mistake from him. But he won't be able to afford many in this field.' In private, she railed against the twelve stone handicap.

Ironically, this race turned out to be one of the highlights of Burrough Hill Lad's career. He surged into the lead across the muddy ground and after a superb leap at the last opened up a twenty length lead – only during the run-in did he start to slow. Given the huge handicap

Burrough Hill Lad carried, it was an astonishing performance.

Timeform concluded, 'Burrough Hill Lad was magnificent in the Hennessy Cognac Gold Cup, jumping fluently throughout and winning in most impressive fashion. We rate his performance – he won by four lengths and twenty from Canny Danny and Gaye Chance – the best seen in a steeplechase since Arkle's day, better than Captain Christy's breathtaking thirty length victory in the 1975 King George VI Chase, which stands out in recent memory.'

John Francome was also effusive in his praise. 'This was Burrough Hill Lad's best race as he was top weight. Jockeys tend to go too soon at Newbury and the fences are unforgiving so you have to be spot on.'

Afterwards, Johnny struck fear into the opposition declaring, 'He'll be even better when he is fit. He's got everything. He must be the best horse I've ever sat on. He's got tremendous courage, stays forever, and you could not find a horse with a better temperament.' He even compared Burrough Hill Lad's performance in the Gold Cup and the Hennessy to the immortal Arkle and mischievously commented, 'Yes, but Arkle was probably fully fit when he did it.'

Jenny Pitman couldn't have agreed more. 'He's improving all the time. God willing the best is yet to come.' High praise indeed. She stayed remarkably relaxed when Burrough Hill Lad appeared a little lame pulling up, knowing in all probability he'd just knocked the scar on his hind leg. Once the nerve endings settled things would improve.

In fact, in the lead up to the race, three of Burrough Hill Lad's legs were in bandages. Pus had been exuding from one of his forefeet and a thorn had become embedded in a hind leg. Despite having only one leg poultice-free, he still produced a defining performance.

There was a real aura surrounding Burrough Hill Lad now. A punter walked into a bookmaker in South London with £12,000 cash and laid the lot on Buzby to win the Gold Cup again.

Next was an easy win at Wetherby for the Charlie Hall Memorial Pattern Chase. Phil Tuck's quiet manner was vindicated; he was asked to ride again and won convincingly by ten lengths. Apart from the last fence, which Burrough Hill Lad hit with some force, it was a faultless race.

The gloss was taken off this victory when Jenny received news that her son Mark had been involved in a car crash. He'd skidded on black ice en route to the course and had to be cut from his vehicle. When Jenny heard he was being taken to Warwick Hospital by ambulance, she naturally dropped everything to be there. At the end of the meeting, everyone felt a little anxious and Kath offered to drive home. She'd passed her test not long before and the novelty had yet to wear off. They were chatting about the day's events when, just a few miles before the Leicester turnoff on the M1, Kath complained she felt a bit dizzy. At first Stan assumed it was a result of the day's stress and was about to suggest they change places. Suddenly Kath slumped over the steering wheel, unconscious. Hurtling down the middle lane of the motorway at seventy miles per hour, it was a life or death situation. Car horns screamed as Stan pushed Kath's limp body aside and struggled to take control of the vehicle.

'I spotted a gap in the traffic in the wing mirror and grabbed the steering wheel,' said Stan. 'I flicked the indicator and steered the motorhome onto the hard shoulder, pulling Kath's foot off the accelerator till we eventually stopped. It all happened very fast, I didn't have much time to think.'

Now they were safe, Stan turned his attention to the woman he loved.

'Kath was semi-conscious and couldn't talk.' He jumped out and dragged her onto the passenger seat, then ran round to the driver's seat. With no mobile phones and the next motorway emergency phone miles away, Stan made another split second decision. 'I had to get help fast but we weren't far from home and I knew where all the hospitals were. I made for those.'

The most obvious destination was the A&E at Leicester Royal Infirmary but they were likely to get held up in the busy arterial routes around the city centre. Precious time would be wasted. Stan gambled and instead drove straight for Groby Road Hospital, where Kath's cardiologist had treated her only three days before. 'They would be right up to date with her heart problems and I didn't want to waste time explaining her condition to doctors at the Royal.'

The relief of arriving at Groby Hospital quickly faded when a receptionist shook her head and tried to divert him back to the Royal Infirmary, stating unequivocally, 'We are not an A&E department.'

Stan was having none of it. 'I point-blank refused to go until they saw Kath. Eventually they agreed and nurses came and wheeled her inside.'

Stan's refusal to take no for an answer saved Kath's life. She had suffered a stroke.

After a stay in hospital, the doctors' advice was un-equivocal: slow down. Kath knew she was lucky to be alive and that she had Stan to thank for it. Surgery to repair her leaking valve was now more urgent than ever. But Kath, still afraid of the procedure, again refused to consent to the operation.

Although seriously shaken by events, Stan had little time to dwell. Burrough Hill Lad was entered at Kempton for the King George VI Chase on Boxing Day, pitching him against his old adversary Wayward Lad and the tal-ented Combs Ditch. When Jenny and Stan met, there was a joint bond: they had both come face to face with the fear of losing a loved one, but the focus had to be the race.

Destined to be a three-horse thriller, from the off the two Lads were neck and neck. It was exactly the sort of race punters had hoped for; hard, scrappy, and nothing between them. Even though Combs Ditch was holding up the rear, he refused to lose touch as the two mighty Lads battled it out. At the final bend, Wayward Lad gradually fell away, unable to respond to further encouragement.

For a moment it appeared Burrough Hill Lad had got the race in the bag until, almost from nowhere, Combs Ditch put in a tremendous effort. By the time they reached the final fence he had not only drawn level but was actually a length in front. The tables turned, Burrough Hill Lad now had to dig deep and Johnny Francome used all his experience to push on. As they approached the line, Burrough Hill Lad straining every sinew, it was still neck and neck. In fact, it was too close to call and a photo finish was announced. The result, to a huge cheer from the crowd, declared Burrough Hill Lad's victory, by the narrowest of margins – a short head.

John Francome had ridden an inspired race. He said, 'I met the second from last spot on and I thought Combs Ditch was going better than me. I pulled my whip though and sat still for four strides and then it was nip and tuck to the line.'

If Burrough Hill Lad was exhausted, so was Stan. That wasn't just close, it was incredible. Somehow, victory tasted sweeter when hard fought for.

Even John looked done in and was in Jenny's bad books for not pushing harder at the start. It also transpired that Jenny, always one to keep a tidy ship, had a bee in her bonnet – she thought Johnny's long curls may be causing problems! She told the press, 'I can't stand his hair. I won't employ lads with earrings and any lad with long hair is told to get it cut at once!'

Everyone needed a break, especially Burrough Hill Lad who appeared very tired afterwards, not helped by the fact he had bitten his tongue during the race. But it was unlikely to happen as they edged ever closer towards the climax of the season. Compensation came in the knowledge that after this appearance, Burrough Hill Lad's prize winnings were a mouth-watering £164,000.

In preparation for the 1985 Gold Cup, Burrough Hill Lad had two more races. First on the agenda was a three miler at Sandown for the prestigious Gainsborough Handicap Chase. Always a fine race with plenty of runners, this year seemed to be no exception. As the big day approached, several chasers dropped out for one reason or another. Such was the power of Burrough Hill Lad that he was frightening off the opposition. Five trainers came up with suitable excuses. Fred Winter said Half Free had not run for several months due to an injury and therefore it wouldn't be fair on the horse. The Queen Mother's Special Cargo pulled up a couple of days beforehand with a knock and trainer Fulke Walwyn wasn't prepared to risk him. And so it went on.

Sandown's Clerk of the Course, Mark Kershaw expressed his disappointment but was at a loss to know what to do. 'I just hope this is no more than a one off disaster,' he said.

On the day, thousands of people were there to watch but only one horse turned up prepared to race: Burrough Hill Lad. John Francome, wearing full colours, cantered down to the start in race tack and to great applause paraded in front of the stand. It was a walkover. Although Stan was pleased to take all the prize money, there was someone who wasn't happy – Burrough Hill Lad. Stan said, 'He didn't like this very much at all. He had been preparing as usual and began performing for his fans on the way down to the start, fully expecting to race, and then was just brought back in again. It seemed to me that Burrough Hill Lad was a bit confused, disappointed and frustrated by it all.'

Stan went on to make his own shock announcement: if the price was right he was finally prepared to sell Burrough Hill Lad. He'd just received an unexpected offer of £200,000, a sizeable sum, but was holding out for more so he could invest the money and become a full-time breeder. The offer had turned his head and, casting all sentiment to the side, Stan thought this was an opportunity to finally secure his future. Time was not on Stan's side. He would have to strike while Buzby's stock was high.

With the Gold Cup just weeks away and Burrough Hill Lad the hottest favourite to win since Arkle, John Francome waxed lyrical about his chances. 'I've never been beaten on Burrough Hill Lad and he's such a horse that I can't believe I ever will. He's 1/2 for the Gold Cup, but strictly on the form book he should be even shorter.'

His main rival, Combs Ditch, was struggling and required emergency treatment after his last race at Ascot. He initially seemed fine, but a few minutes after finishing almost collapsed with breathing problems. The course vet was called to administer drugs and give oxygen.

According to newspapers, Burrough Hill Lad was a likely contender for the Grand National at the end of

March, but Jenny Pitman cast doubt on whether she would approve such a race if Burrough Hill Lad carried top weight of twelve stone five pounds. It was cruel, she said. 'The RSPCA should stop any horse carrying more than twelve stones in the National.' Unless the weight was changed, she was unlikely to sanction Burrough Lad's participation.

As the Gold Cup drew nearer, heavy snowfall made training precarious. It was essential to keep the horse in tip-top condition and warm-up races were hard to come by with meetings cancelled all round the country. Jenny's solution was to take Burrough Hill Lad to the seaside. The temperature was a welcome few degrees warmer at Brean Sands near Burnham-on-Sea and an ideal spot to work the horses. Burrough Hill Lad couldn't have been happier, he loved the miles of soft beach and foaming waves, galloping along the shoreline, blissfully carefree.

Scobie Jones said that whilst the change of scene put everyone in great spirits, the new environment provided all sorts of unknown challenges. 'Burrough Hill Lad was going along in four inches of water – bah-bum, bah-bum – then all of a sudden, what the hell? He'd just galloped across a sunken car – right across the roof. We stopped going down there and started going to Port Talbot instead because there were no cars buried on the beach!'

Desperate for a race prior to the Gold Cup, Burrough Hill Lad entered the Newbury Greenall Whitley Brewers Chase carrying a crushing twelve stone seven pounds. He conceded a mind blowing 29 pounds to second favourite, Earls Brig.

During the first lap, John Francome kept Burrough Hill Lad on the inside. When Richdee and Earls Brig accelerated round the last bend, Burrough Hill Lad was caught flat footed. By the second-last he was twenty lengths behind the leader and never looked likely to make up ground, yet Francome somehow managed to ease him over the line in fourth. Despite murmurs of disapproval from punters who believed Francome had not tried hard enough, Stan's verdict was he'd done his best but been beaten by the weight. Johnny turned all attention back to the horse, 'He ran a cracker, I was delighted with him.'

It made absolutely no difference to the Tote and Burrough Hill Lad's price held at 1/2 to win the Gold Cup. It looked a shoe-in, all he had to do was turn up. Anyone involved in racing will tell you that a dollop of good luck is the prerequisite for success. A mere five days ahead of Cheltenham, Burrough Hill Lad's luck ran out.

During a routine weekend training session, his leg was cut around the inside of his knee. Burrough Hill Lad's idiosyncratic way of running with his head hanging low resulted in his teeth catching on his own leg. It had happened before, but never caused so deep a cut. Jenny immediately called the vet who did everything possible, yet the injury continued to blow up and by Monday morning the horse's chance of competing plummeted.

Every human effort was made to restore Burrough Hill Lad to racing health. They even used a newfangled megapulse machine to stimulate healing, but nothing worked and the bruising persisted. Jenny, who always put a horse's best welfare first, saw absolutely no merit in pushing on and causing long-term damage. She picked up the phone to Stan and told him the bad news. After a brief discussion and with a heavy heart, he withdrew Burrough Hill Lad from the Gold Cup and the Grand National.

Scobie Jones knew the extraordinary lengths they would go to ensure Burrough Hill Lad stayed fit. Yet this time, the miracle they sought eluded even these experienced horsemen and women. It had all come to nothing. 'I used to spend at least three months every year on a hose pipe, half an hour on each shin and half and hour each leg. That was four hours a day for three months of the year, when it was minus ten, snowing, raining, whatever. I'd chuck a load of rugs over him and sit on a bucket with a hose pipe. I'd be there two hours every morning and two hours every night. He had a real bad scar on his off hind and it had healed the wrong way out so all the nerves were on the outside. But when he kicked it, he picked that leg up as high as his arse and would nearly topple over. I was cleaning him out one night and thought "what the hell's that?" and he took the bone out of it. He never had anything on it when he was racing, just when he was walking. Now and again when he was trotting he'd knock it.'

In the peak of form and at the height of his powers, Burrough Hill Lad was counted out. A last-ditch attempt with a specially made boot to heal the wound came to nothing. Nothing could get him fit in time. Vet's orders were to rest over the summer and come back in the autumn. It quickly put paid to any thoughts of Stan selling him.

Weeks turned to months and it was not until the end of November that Burrough Hill Lad raced again. His inaugural run for the season was at Chepstow on the last day of the month in the aptly-named Rehearsal Stakes. Yet again he was pitched against his old adversary, the redoubtable Wayward Lad.

A particularly foggy day, most punters could only see the very last fence. Those watching on television got a better view of what was to be a heart-stopping moment. Burrough Hill Lad powered towards the final fence with a narrow lead. As he approached, no one could tell he was taking off a stride too early. Desperately stretching for the other side of the fence, his hindquarters smacked right into it, unbalancing jockey Phil Tuck.

In a truly skilful piece of riding, Phil leant right back, legs completely extended and gave the reins full length. Burrough Hill Lad landed straight and after a few stuttering strides found a rhythm. He went on to pip West Tip.

Afterwards, Phil looked mightily relieved as he explained Burrough Hill Lad started to tire and had 'guessed' at the fence. Being such a big strong horse this time he got away with it. 'Anyone standing at that fence would have heard some strong language,' he laughed. The joke went round that Phil had superglue on his stirrups. Maybe he had ice in his veins too.

His nineteenth win landed Burrough Hill Lad in the record books – he'd now won more money than any other horse under National Hunt rules, a grand total of £184,095. His performance was even more remarkable considering the extent of his injuries the pervious season. Now the goal was to win the 1986 Gold Cup. In preparation, Jenny wanted to work on Burrough Hill Lad's fitness and lined him up for a couple of December races.

Two weeks before Christmas, the SGB Handicap Chase at Ascot saw a record crowd gather to watch Burrough Hill Lad. He was carrying twelve stone seven pounds, much to Jenny's annoyance. She didn't think he had a chance shouldering that weight and complained, 'I'm not going to have my horse knocked to pieces when he has an impossible task.'

Her prediction came true and Door Latch beat Burrough Hill Lad into third place by eleven lengths. Stan was less downbeat. Yes, his horse was carrying so much extra he'd been unlikely to win, but still Burrough Hill Lad gamely outpaced and overtook fourth-placed The Tsarevich during the run in.

Phil Tuck also dismissed the criticism, certain Burrough Hill Lad's poor jumping had little to do with defeat. 'He brushed through the top of the first and got a bit close to two more, but that was nothing. It was a great performance under twelve stone seven pounds and I'm looking forward to proving that he's better than ever.'

On to Kempton for the Boxing Day showpiece, and an attempt to retain The King George VI Chase against his old adversary, Wayward Lad. After leading for the majority of the race, Burrough Hill Lad started to blow hard and fell off the pace from just two fences out. Aside from a couple of minor jumping errors, he seemed to run out of steam. Stan valiantly tried to shrug off Buzby's lacklustre performance as a case of post Christmas blues!

Timeform commented, 'Burrough Hill Lad gave a performance wholly out of character, a well beaten fourth in the King George VI Chase at Kempton on Boxing Day. Normally a sound jumper and thoroughly game and genuine he married his performance with two serious mistakes and found very little off the bridle, fading tamely when headed by the winner Wayward Lad at the second last. Burrough Hill Lad impressed enormously in appearance, as he usually does, and his display was inexplicable.'

Deep down, Stan couldn't get that meet out of his head, especially when rumblings began again about another race being thrown. Kath was quoted saying Phil Tuck had failed to follow their orders. 'We told him to go on and make all if it was a slow pace, but he didn't and that's why he made those jumping errors.'

Stan took the brunt of some pretty heavy criticism from the racing press. John Oaksey went as far as to suggest 'good horses do not always get the owners they deserve' and argued Phil Tuck was being blamed for something that wasn't his fault. If Burrough Hill Lad failed to perform it was down to other factors, he thought.

Phil kept his head down while the controversy raged, stating he preferred to get on with racing. He may have been more forthcoming had he known that was to be the last time he would ever ride Burrough Hill Lad. Over the next few days Stan concluded they needed to switch things up a little. This time he called in Peter Scudamore. 'I feel sorry for Phil,' Peter said, 'but history relates that if I turned down the ride it would be offered to someone else.'

It fell to Timeform to focus on the facts of the matter. 'Sensationalised stories are always good for filling and selling newspapers, but the principle surely has to be accepted that an owner has the perfect right to put up anyone he wishes on his horse, the law of the land and the Rules Of Racing permitting.'

Jenny immediately invited Peter Scudamore to Lambourn to school the ten year old. He duly arrived the day before the race after picking John Francome's brain on the best way to ride Burrough Hill Lad. 'John told me not to let go of his head, because that was when me made mistakes. If you just sat still and kept hold of his head he would sort himself out and keep running.'

Scudamore developed a special 'squeezing and lengthening' technique with Burrough Hill Lad for better preparation approaching a fence. It also allowed him to ease him back on his hocks to jump.

Scobie Jones had his own theory on Burrough Hill Lad's individual running and jumping style. 'He was an absolute machine. I used to have a solid nickel bit and he tugged it so hard, he bent it. He'd come up the straight and we'd turn up the big steep hill where he'd drop the bit, turn around and look to see what was working with him.

If anything got near, he'd pick the bit up and go again. He was a dream. I'd always say, "Kick him into every fence because if you leave him alone he'll muller it." When he's running, he's lobbing along and his ears swing, one-two, one-two, back and forwards they swing, going at opposite times, then as soon as he puts the peddle down those two ears go flat back. That's when he starts racing.'

As a warm-up ride ahead of the Gold Cup, Jenny Pitman settled on the Gainsborough Handicap Chase at Sandown on 1 February. For a while, this meeting looked like it may have to be abandoned due to a waterlogged course, then at the last minute a £4,000 machine known as a waterhog sucked up all the excess water. It tipped the balance and kept the meeting open. The soft going was in Burrough Hill Lad's favour.

Through the bitter cold, the race kept exactly to plan with Burrough Hill Lad storming back into form and a magnificent ten lengths victory.

Scobie Jones witnessed every twist and turn that day. 'When Scudamore was riding him going down the back straight he was probably thinking, if I get beaten on this they're going to call me all the names under the sun. He's scrubbing away thinking, Jesus Christ he's not going to pick up for me. Then I saw them coming along the bottom bend, he jumped the bottom fence and his ears went flat back and he just picked up, won it by ten lengths. Scudamore said to me, "He frightened the shit out of me, you didn't tell me he did that!" He thought the horse was going to do him.'

Afterwards, Peter Scudamore and Phil Tuck were seen chatting like old mates, proving there really were no hard feelings. 'He's a smashing fella,' Phil said.

At the end of the month the cold weather kicked in with a vengeance leaving the Lambourn gallops once again unusable. Jenny Pitman loaded up her horses and drove back to the beach at Port Talbot. After enforced rest it was vital Burrough Hill Lad kept ticking over. He was in such good form, no one wanted his fitness to drop before the Cheltenham Festival. Burrough Hill Lad, ever adaptable, took to the sea and surrounding sands as if born there.

In the lead up to the Gold Cup, the Pitman camp suddenly fell quiet. Silence, to the journalists, meant something was up. This time they were right. Five days before the Gold Cup the awful news broke. Burrough Hill Lad was injured. It looked like he was about to be withdrawn from the race for the second year in succession.

After 1985, this was beyond bad luck. To be struck down at exactly the same point was appalling misfortune. Two years running, Burrough Hill Lad had been at the top of his game and clear favourite, yet with just days to go his body defeated him. His legs had literally let him down.

Chasing round for a controversial angle is the stock-in-trade of newspapers and trainer Mick Easterby appeared to condemn Burrough Hill Lad's recent trip to Wales. 'Beaches are death traps, I wouldn't dream of exercising any of my horses on sand.'

Peter Scudamore, booked to ride Burrough Hill Lad, refused to cast aspersions. 'The beach exercise has nothing to do with it. It was probably the revival of an old injury.'

Jenny eventually revealed the truth. Burrough Hill Lad was battling 'heat' in his off foreleg – swelling around the tendons and tissues. The last thing she wanted was the ten year old to break down or become so badly injured he was unable to race again. There was nothing for it. Burrough Hill Lad was dropped from the Gold Cup and sent to rest for the remainder of the season. Jenny remained optimistic, saying, 'There is still a bit of mileage in him.' Everybody hoped so.

'At his best, he is in a league of his own among contemporary staying chasers,' wrote Timeform. 'As in 1985, he was ante-post favourite for the Gold Cup at the time of his enforced withdrawal. Leg trouble is expected to keep Burrough Hill Lad off the course until the second part of the 1986-7 season.'

They urged appreciation over quick judgement. 'Relish it while it lasts, for, make no mistake, steeplechasers of Burrough Hill Lad's brilliance are seen rarely.'

One question remained on everyone's lips. Was there more to come?

12

Burrough Hill Lad's career hung in the balance. He had not competed for over a year and his delicate legs needed constant attention. Stan was seriously worried and had to turn his hand to whatever would bring in some cash – the bills were still landing on his doormat.

'He was almost sixty and this was the first time he'd not worked for himself,' said Sue, 'so it was very strange for him. He bagged up a bit of horse muck for local gardeners. Then he tried all sorts of things, such as selling magnetic bracelets for their health benefits, making miniature grandfather clocks and selling limited edition prints of a Burrough Hill Lad painting, but none of these ideas made him much so he was living off his rapidly depleting savings.'

In desperation he delivered televisions to Birmingham, just to keep his head above water. In the meantime, he continued trying to maximise Burrough Hill Lad's fame.

Following the Gold Cup win, Stan had been advised there was a lucrative market for equine memorabilia. 'Give them something to remember the horse by,' he was told. 'A lovely little piece of history.' With those encouraging words ringing in his ears, Stan filed an application to register Burrough Hill Lad as a trademark using Serjeants, specialist patent lawyers in Leicester. They in turn sought guidance from the agent who had marketed Red Rum. The fee was almost a thousand pounds, but with those kind of credentials, Stan considered it a worthwhile investment.

A letter popped through Stan's door by return post. He ripped open the envelope hopeful of good news. A quick scan revealed the situation was fraught with legal complications.

Serjeants wrote, 'because the Trademark Red Rum was applied for when the horse was already famous, the Trade Marks Registry had objected to the Applications for Registration of Red Rum on the basis that any trader in the UK should be allowed to use that famous name. This suggests that it is desirable to file the Application for "Burrough Hill Lad" early, before this stage is reached.'

Ironically, the more famous Burrough Hill Lad became, the less likely he was to be granted a trademark.

Commercially it made no sense to keep Burrough Hill Lad's name out of the spotlight. If Stan was going to make any money out of this venture, he needed his horse to become a household name. The very exclusivity he sought was jeopardising the deal. It was a catch-22.

Not one to give up easily, Stan pressed on. Each day he awoke emboldened by a new idea. First it was Burrough Hill Lad statuettes and figurines, then horse shoes, then printed matter. After a trip round a DIY store he came up with ceramic or earthenware articles including decorative tiles. Now he had grandchildren, how about Burrough Hill Lad toys and games and playthings? Stan hoped with a bit of luck and the right marketing his horse could be part of the racing zeitgeist, up there with Red Rum and Arkle. Stan became fixated on doing everything in his power to ensure he retained ownership of Burrough Hill Lad's name. It didn't seem right others could profit from all his hard work.

As the season progressed, other matters became more pressing. Kath's health was in decline; her heart condition worsened and doctors struggled to find a remedy. It once again put life into perspective. Finding time to wade through the legal minefield of copyright and trademarks became irrelevant, something he'd save for a rainy day. He put the papers away in a drawer and sought the advice of a financial adviser for more traditional ways to secure their future. The stock market boomed throughout 1986 and the first part of 1987, so Stan invested a good proportion of his winnings into the FTSE 100. Never having dabbled in stocks or shares in his life, this was a totally new venture and a complete departure from Stan's small business sensibilities. The promise was a healthy nest egg to carry him through old age.

At first all went well and Stan's portfolio yielded a decent profit. He sat back and watched his money grow. But Stan should have known there's no such thing as a sure bet.

On Monday 19 October 1987, the financial markets collapsed.

Between a quarter and a half of the value of investors' assets were wiped out in a single day. Stan watched helpless as his life savings crumble away. He felt utterly out of control, panicked and powerless.

What had he done? And what should he do next?

The bullish view was to sit tight and wait for the market to calm down. But Stan was a child of the depression years brought up with stories of the Wall Street Crash in 1929 and the years of austerity that followed. He had to act; that was his nature. Contacting his broker, Stan told him to sell everything – immediately. 'Don't wait,' he said. 'Get out before it gets any worse.'

Despite firm advice to the contrary, Stan wanted nothing more to do with the world of financial markets. But sell-sell-sell turned out to be a decision he lived to regret. Within a few weeks, after all his stocks had been withdrawn, the market started to slowly recover. There's no question Stan's timing was lousy. Any hope of the security he envisaged disappeared, literally overnight. He was go-

ing to have to drag himself away from potential bankruptcy on the back of Burrough Hill Lad's mighty shoulders.
They'd done it before and could do it again.

Another season's racing, feeling his whole life depend-
ed upon one horse, brought huge pressure. Yet Stan kept
his nightmare financial situation secret.

Back in Lambourn, Jenny Pitman kept a careful eye
on Buzby, getting him as close to race fit as could be.
Jenny allowed Christmas to come and go as she nursed
Burrough Hill Lad patiently through one training session
after another. Everything about Burrough Hill Lad suggested there was more to come. He was still strong, powerful and competitive. Jenny refused to be rushed.

As it had now been over two years since his last race
and wanting to give him every opportunity, Jenny took
Burrough Hill Lad to Wincanton for the Jim Ford Challenge Cup. This was a race with good memories. He'd
won here four years previously as a prelude to Gold Cup
victory. Fully rested and raring to go, if he did well there
was an outside chance of running in the next Gold Cup.
Stan arrived, hopeful and nervous as ever. With three to
go the signs were good. Burrough Hill Lad was in contention right next to Desert Orchid. He jumped well and his
speed over the flat had not noticeably diminished. Ridden
for the first time by Richard Rowe, it looked like the old
Lad was back.

Until his foibles returned to haunt him. Buzby may
have been a little older, but he could not claim to be wiser.
He mistimed the fence, hit it hard and stuttered for a mo-

ment as he tried to regain his stride. The stuffing knocked out of him, his confidence gone, Burrough Hill Lad faded towards the back of the field.

Ring rusty, he was going to need more races to get back up to speed. Sadly, the years away had not restored him to his former glory. His legs were now not only a little older, they were suffering from having been patched up many times. Like a punch-drunk boxer, it was hard to get back up. The limbs ached more than ever and injuries took much longer to repair. It all made him a little more tentative.

Ever optimistic, Jenny Pitman kept smiling and said she was pleased with his run. 'I felt certain that the next time out we'd see the old Burrough Hill Lad again.'

Then, just three weeks later, he pulled up during a workout at Newbury. It was obvious his legs were in a state.

Although hugely disappointed, Jenny also admitted she was relieved. Having to constantly patch up Burrough Hill Lad was tough. Every horse in that yard was like one of her babies and she looked after them as if they were her own kids. Scobie Jones said they all felt the weight of responsibility. 'We all had to do our job properly and then there was no problem. But if you didn't by God you knew about it!'

However realistic the potential for ongoing success, it would be unfair and unkind to keep pushing Burrough Hill Lad only to risk provoking old injuries.

Scobie Jones agreed. He'd started riding Burrough Hill Lad with fingers crossed. 'We used a gallop called the Bowl and he'd start off at the bottom, come down through a bit of a dip, go back up to the tree, then have three-quarters of a mile round the Bowl and back down through that dip. Every time my heart was in my mouth because I knew what his legs were like and I'd think, "Don't you dare break down, don't you dare!" But by the end it was like doing seventy miles per hour on a clapped out Rolls-Royce.'

Although he loved Buzby, he also knew his time was up. It had been a privilege to be involved with such a brilliant beast. 'When you get a horse like that, they're one in a million, you're lucky if you get one of them in a lifetime.'

Jenny and Stan discussed Burrough Hill Lad's future, coming at it from every conceivable angle. Neither could see how he would race again. It was a difficult conversation as both acknowledged the end of an era. They had been through so much together and Burrough Hill Lad had given his all. Now it was over and there was very little left to say.

There was also one final issue to resolve: Stan owed Jenny almost two thousand pounds in stable fees, money he was hard pressed to find. Unable to think of a better way round the situation he offered her a practical solution – you have Burrough Hill Lad and we'll call it quits on the cash. Jenny agreed in a heartbeat.

Stan didn't want to prolong the painful process. He owned no land and according to Sue, 'didn't like the idea of Burrough Hill Lad just being put in a field and living out the rest of his days getting bored and fat, which is probably what would have happened if Dad had tried to keep him.'

Stan wanted the best for his horse and there was no doubt in his mind Jenny was the perfect owner. So they shook hands and he walked away, never looking back.

'I only wanted the best retirement possible for Burrough Hill Lad,' said Stan. 'I was very relieved when Jenny agreed to take him, not to pay off my account, but because I knew she was the one person who would do their very best by him.'

Sue was also deeply saddened. 'His career was brought to a premature end entirely due to his leg injuries. If he could have run another race, then he surely would have done. He was quite young to retire really, as chasers typically go on until they're fourteen years old and a few have continued to win races even aged eighteen. It was a great shame he couldn't continue.'

If he had raced, the risk would be that he would break down completely with a serious, irreparable injury which could, worst case scenario, lead to having to be put down. 'Neither Dad nor Jenny would ever have taken that risk. Burrough Hill Lad owed them nothing.'

Stan reflected on the remarkable horse that had put him in the history books. 'I was very, very proud of Burrough Hill Lad,' he said. 'He was the best horse I ever had and better than any I could ever have dreamt of having, let alone owning and breeding. I loved riding him when he was at home. I always knew that it wouldn't go on forever, and that one day it would all come to an end. It was a shame it was early, but even so, I was just grateful for the time and fun I had with him. It is true that I didn't look back or go to say goodbye to Burrough Hill Lad when I left him at Jenny's. But I've always hated goodbyes and wouldn't have wanted to make a fuss about it, but that doesn't mean I didn't care about him. We'd been through a lot together.'

13

Burrough Hill Lad's racing days had finally drawn to an end, his legs unable to do as his heart demanded. But it was also a new beginning for Buzby.

With his racing years behind him he'd earned a tranquil retirement, a place where his speed and good looks would be welcomed. He'd been handled with kid gloves most of his life, provided with the best money could buy, and deserved a decent, loving home in his golden years.

Jenny consulted her bulging contacts book and after a short-term loan to a hunting friend, Burrough Hill Lad was offered to a landowner in Yorkshire.

Charlie Warde-Aldam, master of Badsworth Fox Hunt, was always on the look out for good horses. And being friends with Jenny's younger sister, Mandy, meant he could be relied upon. They had known each other for years and Jenny trusted his judgement while he respected her knowledge. Charlie recalled, 'Jenny phoned me up and said would I consider looking after old Buzby. I thought about it for all of one second then said, "Yes, by all means, the waggon's on its way." '

However, there were some very specific stipulations. It was clear Charlie was on for a heck of a challenge.

'Jenny told me three things,' said Charlie. 'One: treat him as your own – she had enough respect for how I looked after horses. Two: he will make matchsticks of any timber fence. And three: when he bucks in Lambourn you can see Swindon town centre! I thought, great!'

Sue was absolutely thrilled. 'It turned out Stan's decision was right,' she said. 'Jenny found him a home where he was very well looked after, appreciated and able to fully participate in a sport which he would no doubt thoroughly enjoy. Dad had no regrets.'

For a long time Charlie kept quiet about his new arrival. He didn't want people sniffing around trying to discover the whereabouts of the former Gold Cup champion when there was work for him to do. If nobody suspected Burrough Hill Lad's identity he was much more likely to be left in peace.

'I didn't tell anyone, it avoided any expectations. If you didn't know, you'd just think this big black handsome animal was an old-fashioned thoroughbred.'

Charlie and Burrough Hill Lad immediately bonded, there was a trust between them. 'He never bucked me off, although he had a go,' Charlie said. 'I think I was the only person he never removed. We soon had a good understanding. I rode him with double bridle so I had all the severity or softness I needed and he never touched a fence. We just clicked.'

Any other riders were told to expect the unexpected. 'I only put decent riders on him, but warned them they'd be bucked. As long as they were prepared to put up with that, it was fine. That was the privilege of riding such a quality horse,' said Charlie.

Charlie discovered Burrough Hill Lad had a unique way of letting riders know he was about to buck.

'There were three revolutions of the tail then up came the backside. It came up so far his front end went backwards. He then pulled his front end from underneath you, so you actually went over and landed on your feet in front of him – he'd be staring at the back of your head.'

After a settling in period, Charlie couldn't resist testing Burrough Hill Lad to see if he was still and strong and fast as he looked. After all, he was not the kind of horse you could leave to just wander about the paddock. To get the best from him, Buzby needed constant stimulation and a good deal of exercise. Ironically, the poor health of one of the staff led to Burrough Hill Lad being called into action.

'One day my huntsman was ill so I had to pick up the horn. I thought bugger it, I'll hunt the hounds off Buzby,' said Charlie.

Immediately he was aware of how much power this prize racehorse still possessed. Despite his age and old injuries, there was still amazing acceleration.

'He was like riding an old, high-powered vehicle. You could feel the size of the engine, but the one trouble was, you've got a flat tyre,' said Charlie. 'When you were cantering you didn't feel you were moving at any great speed but then you'd look about you and all the others were scrubbing like buggery to keep up with you.'

After that there could be no hiding this horse. It was obvious he was extraordinary. Charlie came clean and admitted he was riding a Gold Cup champion. 'I had every point-to-pointer in Yorkshire coming up beside me to see how good he was. He knew he was special. Like that Chelsea manager, José Mourinho, except Buzby would have told you more subtly he was the special one.'

Burrough Hill Lad had a further star turn left: an appearance at the Great Yorkshire Show in 1998 where Charlie proudly rode him. 'He was 22 and I thought that was fitting.'

He then took him around racecourses and used his drawing power to raise money for charity and the St John Ambulance. Charlie got accustomed to the stares and comments as people marvelled at Burrough Hill Lad. It was as if they'd seen some sort of super horse.

'I took him to Cheltenham and he was in the paddock with the Gold Cup runners and we had to take him out because the punters saw the other horses and he still looked the fittest.'

Charlie knew that beneath the facade of the big beast, Buzby was a gentle animal that wouldn't hurt a fly. Shortly after one charity event he was reunited with Jenny and it was like they had never been apart.

'Jenny took him out of the ring and he stood while they fed him Polos. He was a complete lamb. I'd have the kids round about him and made no exceptions for how he behaved.'

Then, one day just before Christmas 2003, Burrough Hill Lad showed the telltale signs of old age. Despite encouragement, he refused to get up. A little while later, much to everyone's relief he clambered up and walked himself around. But something was not right. Within three weeks he was off his feet again, looking very tired. Charlie now faced the inevitable. The great champion's life was drawing to a close.

Within days the decision was made. 'I put him down myself,' said Charlie. 'I wouldn't let anyone else do it,'

Burrough Hill Lad's final resting place was chosen for its beauty and tranquillity. 'He's buried under a big rubbing stone in front of the park alongside two other horses I had,' said Charlie.

Despite Burrough Hill Lad not having raced for almost two decades, he was far from forgotten. Newspapers reported his life with great affection. He wasn't just a winner; he was a great character, all that strength and determination singling him out from other champions. Jenny Pitman said at his peak he resembled 'a Rolls-Royce against stock cars'. Yet his greatest victories were completed with just one good leg. He was, in a word, extraordinary.

To Sue, he will always be Black Beauty, a magnificent horse that not just catapulted her into a different world but brought her family closer. He was the glue that held them together.

When Stan heard the news, he walked slowly to the mantle piece of his Cropston bungalow. Above the fireplace hung paintings and pictures of the horse he had bred and raced. They took pride of place. Each held a special memory of the moments he treasured with Burrough Hill Lad. He may not like to be thought of as a sentimental man, but that day he took out a locked box of memorabilia, sat quietly in his chair overlooking the fields and flipped open the clasp. Towards the bottom, beneath the fading photographs, he found a small plastic wallet. Inside, he felt for a swirl of black coarse hair cut from Burrough Hill Lad's mane, as dark and rich as the day Stan clung to it and galloped across the fields in the village that bears his name.

It had lain there for almost twenty years, untouched. Until that day.

EPILOGUE

Many of racing's biggest names were touched by Burrough Hill Lad.

John Francome was first paid £15 to ride professionally and went on to notch up 1,138 winners, the last in April 1985. Despite ten rides, he never won the Grand National. Soon after retiring, Francome was awarded an MBE for services to racing. He became a trainer for eighteen months before moving on to have a successful broadcasting career. He now enjoys life away from the spotlight and spends much of his time as a successful author and property developer. 'I'm an odd job man, a navvy,' he jokes. Francome was Champion Jockey seven times, and ranks as the third most successful National Hunt jump jockey, only beaten by Tony McCoy and another of Burrough Hill Lad's jockeys, Peter Scudamore.

'Scu' was Champion Jockey eight times and rode 1,678 winners. Like Francome, he was awarded an MBE for services to racing. After retiring from the saddle in 1993, at the age of 34, he began a career in journalism. He now lives and trains with his partner, Lucinda Russell, at their Arlary House Stables in Scotland. A successful broadcaster, Scudamore writes a regular newspaper column. His son Michael has a yard in Herefordshire while other son Tom is a jockey.

Jenny Pitman was the first female trainer to win the Gold Cup with Burrough Hill Lad in 1984. She was also became the first woman to train a Grand National winner, when Corbiere took the victory in 1983. Jenny won the Grand National again with Royal Athlete in 1995 but was denied a further victory with Esha Ness in 1993 when the race was voided following two false starts. Jenny was diagnosed with thyroid cancer in 1997 and is now Patron of the British Thyroid Foundation. She was the first ever winner of the Helen Rollason award at the BBC Sports Personality of the Year Awards in 1999 and retired the same year on the opening day of the Cheltenham Festival. She later became a successful novelist. She has two sons from her first marriage to Champion Jockey, Richard Pitman: Mark is a former jockey, trainer and racehorse buyer while Paul lives and works in Dubai. Jenny lives with her second husband, David Strait, in Berkshire.

Burrough Hill Lad also privileged the lives of those who not only considered him a racehorse, but part of the family.

Margaret, Stan's former wife, died aged 75 in July 2004. Doctors discovered Margaret was suffering from an enlarged aorta. Sue explained, 'A doctor said without treatment she would pass out and be dead within the hour. Mum was okay with that. She was at home when it happened. She was a very brave woman.' Stan paid his respects at her funeral and said how proud he was that Margaret gave him three fine children.

Kath decided to have the operation she had long resisted to treat her heart condition in 2007. She had lived long enough with the threat of a heart attack hanging over her. 'With advances in modern surgical procedures they were able to perform a successful double bypass, using a vein from her leg,' Sue said. 'She was so happy and felt so much better. When we picked her up from Glenfield Hospital, she said, "Don't take me home, take me to the pub, we're having a steak!" After all those years fearing the operation, she was so pleased to be living the other side of it. We went to Woodhouse Eaves. "It's my treat, no arguments," she said. After the nice slap up meal we called into the medical centre in Loughborough so she could say, "Look I've done it and I'm still here!"

'A few weeks later Dad and Kath were getting ready to go shopping. Kath was in the bedroom. Suddenly she cried out "my head, my head" and passed out on the bed. Dad rang 999 and the ambulance came and took her to hospital but she never regained consciousness. She'd suffered a fatal brain haemorrhage. Dad was heartbroken, totally devastated. He phoned me from the hospital in shock. It was terrible. She was the one.

'For the next six months he couldn't stay in the bungalow on his own. He came to my house then would say, "I have to get back to the bungalow. But you've got to come with me." So I camped there with my daughter for weeks. After Kath died it was the first time he'd been on his own in eighty years. Kath was such a big part of his life, she organised everything. They were always together.'

There was no doubting over the years Stan had mellowed. He even expressed a desire to wed. 'He would say to Kath, "Will you marry me?" Kath would always reply, "If it ain't broke, why fix it?" That was her philosophy. Life was just fine the way it was.'

Robert Stanley Riley still lives in the bungalow he bought with Kath, surrounded by her homemade soft furnishings and pictures of Burrough Hill Lad. Now in his eighties, he still likes to follow the hunt with his daughter and granddaughter.

Sue Riley lives just a few minutes away from her father. They see each other regularly and will never forget the big black horse that changed all their lives. For Sue, the years with Buzby were special, they defined the bond with her father that lives on to this very day.

'Burrough Hill Lad was a fantastic horse and the memories I have are as much to do with the time I spent with

Dad and Kath. Half of me looked forward to the racing days simply to be out sharing it with them.'

Burrough Hill Lad remains buried in Yorkshire, his resting place still tranquil. Yet he continues to win plaudits – *Racing Post* named him their 44th favourite racehorse in a poll, while Timeform rank him as the eighth best steeplechaser of all time. Not bad for the little black foal born of a rescued mother, raised by a simple farmer's lad in Leicestershire.

Burrough Hill
Lad's Racing Career

Trainer: Jimmy Harris

27 October 1979, Jockey Phil Tuck.
Huntingdon, Cromwell Novices' Hurdle (3y), 2m 200y.
Eighth.

3 November 1979, Jockey Gordon Holmes.
Wetherby, Thorp Arch Novices' Hurdle (3y), 2m.
Thirteenth.

15 November 1979, Jockey Phil Tuck.
Stratford, Southern Cross Novices' Hurdle (3y), 2m.
Third.

19 December 1979, Jockey Phil Tuck.
Warwick, Hampton Maiden Hurdle (3y), 2m.
DNF (pulled up lame after third).

26 December 1979, Jockey Jonathan Haynes.
Market Rasen, Accurate Junior Novices' Hurdle, 2m.
DNF (unseated rider).

5 January 1980, Jockey Phil Tuck.
Market Rasen, Grimsby Novices' Hurdle (4y), 2m.
Winner.

8 January 1980, Jockey Peter Scudamore.
Leicester, Croxton Park Novices' Hurdle (4y), 2m.
Winner.

18 January 1980, Jockey Steve Knight.
Kempton, Royal Mail Handicap Hurdle, 3m.
DNF (fell at last).

28 March 1980, Jockey Phil Tuck.
Liverpool, Maghull Novices' Hurdle, 2m 5f 110y.
Sixth.

5 April 1980, Jockey Phil Tuck.
Southwell, Easter-Egg Handicap Hurdle, 2½m.
Second.

1980-1981 (four year old)
Trainer: Harry Wharton

11 Oct 1980, Jockey Phil Tuck.
Uttoxeter, Stafford Regiment Challenge Cup Hcap Hurdle, 2m 4f.
Winner.

22 October 1980, Jockey Phil Tuck.
Cheltenham, EC Burton Handicap Hurdle, 3m 1f.
Winner.

1981-1982 (five year old)
Trainer: Jenny Pitman

18 November 1981, Jockey Phil Tuck.
Kempton, November Handicap Hurdle, 3m.
Fifth.

27 November 1981, Jockey Phil Tuck.
Newbury, Round Oak Handicap Hurdle, 2m 4f.
Sixth.

4 January 1982, Jockey Phil Tuck.
Nottingham, Nottingham Champion Novices' Chase, 2m 6f.
Seventh.

25 January 1982, Jockey Phil Tuck.
Leicester, Cottesmere Novices' Chase, 3m.
Second.

16 February 1982, Jockey Colin Brown.
Newton Abbot, Rippon Tor Novices' Chase, 3m 2f 100y.
Winner.

6 Mar 1982, Jockey Colin Brown.
Haydock, Mad Hatter Novices' Chase, 3 m 1f.
DNF (unseated rider at fourteenth).

17 March 1982, Jockey Colin Brown.
Cheltenham, Sun Alliance Chase, 3 m.
DNF (fell at sixth).

1 April 1982, Jockey Phil Tuck.
Liverpool, Siematic Kitchen Novices' Chase, 2m 1f.
Winner.

12 April 1982, Jockey Phil Tuck.
Newton Abbot, Foxwell Novices' Chase, 3m 2f 100y.
Winner.

<u>1982-1983 (six year old)</u>
Trainer: Jenny Pitman

23 October 1982, Jockey Phil Tuck.
Stratford, Sean Graham Chase, 3m 2f.
Winner.

30 October 1982, Jockey Phil Tuck.
Ascot, Lambert & Butler Premier Chase Qualifier, 2m 4f.
Winner.

24 November 1982, Jockey Phil Tuck.
Haydock, Edward Hanmer Memorial Chase, 3m.
Second.

<u>1983-1984 (seven year old)</u>
Trainer: Jenny Pitman

10 December 1983, Jockey Ben de Haan.
Nottingham, Coral Golden Handicap Hurdle, 2¾m.
Third.

22 December 1983, Jockey John Francome.
Chepstow, Coral Welsh National, 3¾ miles.
Winner.

7 January 1984, Jockey John Francome.
Sandown, Anthony Mildmay Peter Cazlet Memorial Hcap Chase,
3m 5f 18y.
Winner.

4 February 1984, Jockey John Francome.
Sandown, Gainsborough Handicap Chase, 3m 118y.
Winner.

23 February 1984, Jockey John Francome.
Wincanton, Jim Ford Challenge Cup Chase, 3m 1f.
Winner.

15 March 1984, Jockey Phil Tuck.
Cheltenham, Tote Cheltenham Gold Cup Chase, 3¼m.
Winner.

1984-1985 (eight year old)
Trainer: Jenny Pitman

9 November 1984, Jockey Phil Tuck.
Cheltenham, Standard Life Handicap Chase, 3m.
Third.

16 November 1984, Jockey Phil Tuck.
Wincanton, Silver Buck Handicap Chase, 3m 1f.
Winner.

24 November 1984, Jockey John Francome.
Newbury, Hennessy Cognac Gold Cup, 3¼m.
Winner.

8 December 1984, Jockey Phil Tuck.
Wetherby, Charlie Hall Memorial, 3m 100y.
Winner.

26 December 1984, Jockey John Francome.
Kempton, King George VI Chase, 3m.
Winner.

2 February 1985, Jockey John Francome.
Sandown, Gainsborough Handicap Chase, 3m 118y.
Winner (walkover).

2 March 1985, Jockey Phil Tuck.
Haydock, Greenall Whitley Breweries Handicap Chase, 3m.
Fourth.

1985-1986 (nine year old)
Trainer: Jenny Pitman

30 November 1985, Jockey Phil Tuck.
Chepstow, Rehearsal Chase, 3m.
Winner.

14 December 1985, Jockey Phil Tuck.
Ascot, SGB Handicap Chase, 3m.
Third.

26 December 1985, Jockey Phil Tuck.
Kempton, King George VI Chase.
Fourth.

1 February 1986, Jockey Peter Scudamore.
Sandown, Gainsborough Handicap Chase.
Winner.

1986-1987 (ten year old)
Trainer: Jenny Pitman

Did not race.

1987-1988 (eleven year old)
Trainer: Jenny Pitman

25 February 1988, Jockey Richard Rowe.
Wincanton, Jim Ford Challenge Cup, 3m 1f.
Third.

Total races: 42
Total wins: 22

Acknowledgements

Special thanks go to Sue and Gort Measey, who kindly contacted us when they discovered Burrough Hill Lad had been born in what is now their office. They got the ball rolling, showed us great hospitality and gave us the chance to stay in their stables. The hook where Burrough Hill Lad was tethered still survives!

We knew we were on the right lines when Jenny Pitman told us a book on Burrough Hill Lad and Stan 'for many years had been sadly overlooked'.

Without the indomitable Stan Riley and his daughter Sue Riley, this book could never have been written. Both Stan and Sue put up with our barrage of questions over many hours and always answered patiently and honestly. Sue's Victoria sponge made these meetings even more of a pleasure for us!

We spoke to some of racing's finest including Johnny Francome, Phil Tuck, Ronnie Longford, Mick Bailey, Andrew Scobie Jones, Steve Knight, Charlie Warde-Aldam, Ann Harris and John Harris.

We would also like to thank everyone in the beautiful village of Burrough on the Hill, including the remarkable Bill Fryer, Angela Thorpe, Sherrin Lloyd, Derek Cooper, Sheila Hughes, Trevor Riley, and Dawn Wilson from Burrough Court for their fascinating insights into the area, memories of Burrough Hill Lad and Stan's story.

In Ireland, Sanda Craik-White of Mobarnane House and Paula Murphy of Parkstown House uncovered the proverbial needle in a haystack and offered valuable knowledge with good humour.

The staff at Melton Mowbray Library, Jonathan Stebbing at the Ernest Cook Trust, the British Cheese Board, Ashley Rumney, David Toft and Rodney Pettinga at Raceform in Newbury, and Timeform.

Finally, thanks to our families and friends, for keeping us going, to Pam for reading and suggestions, Tom for all things medical, Holly and Oscar and Ronnie B.

INDEX

Canny Danny 171, 191
Charlie Hall Memorial Pattern Chase 192
Cheltenham 131, 133, 159-161, 163, 165-167, 170, 173, 187, 199, 206, 221, 224, 229-230
Cheltenham Gold Cup 155, 159, 185, 232
Chepstow 150, 154, 201, 231, 233
Cheseldyne Farm 22, 28, 42, 47, 52, 62-63
Combs Ditch 194-195, 197
Corbiere 2, 125-126, 140, 150, 156, 164, 186, 224
Cromwell Novices' Hurdle 121, 228
Croxton Park Novices' Hurdle 125, 229

de Haan, Ben 159, 231
Desert Orchid 212
Door Latch 202
Drop's O'brandy 140
Drumlargan 171, 172

Earls Brig 199
Easterby, Mick 206
Edward Hanmer Memorial Chase 152, 231
Ernest Cook Trust 52, 54, 63, 92-93, 95, 235

Foxwell Novices' Chase 142, 230
Francome, John 151, 154, 156-160, 172, 174, 188-191, 195-197, 199, 204, 223-224, 231-232, 235
Fryer, Bill 24, 35, 75, 170, 235

Gainsborough Chase 156, 196, 205, 231-233
Gaye Chance 191
Greenall, Margaret 'Migs' 113

Green Monkey 77-82, 103-105, 107-108, 114
Grimsby Novices' Hurdle 123, 229

Harris, Ann 115, 118, 129, 235
Harris, Jimmy 3, 114-116, 119-123, 126, 129-131, 228
Haydock 153, 230-232
Haynes, Jonathan 122, 229
Hennessy Gold Cup 166, 188-191, 232
Holmes, Gordon 121, 228
Huntingdon 115, 121, 228

Ison, Geoff 112

Jim Ford Challenge 159, 212, 231, 233

Kempton 1, 3, 125, 130, 140, 194, 202-203, 229-233
Kennelly, John 68
King George VI Chase 191, 194, 202-203, 232-233
Knight, Steve 1-2, 125, 229, 235

Leicester 124, 140, 189, 192-193, 209, 229-230
Lewin, Ena 31, 75
Longford, Ronnie 126-127, 235

Marco Polo 74
Market Rasen 120, 122-124, 229
Matthews, Harry 54, 131
Merry Legs 74

Newbury 140, 188, 191, 198, 213, 230, 232, 235
Newbury Greenall Whitley Brewers Chase 198
Newton Abbot 140, 142, 230
Nottingham 140, 154, 230-231

INNOVATIVE AND EXCITING SPORTS BOOKS

Chequered Flag
PUBLISHING

www.chequeredflagpublishing.co.uk